The First Page

It's my hope that you have decided to read this page before you spend your hard-earned commission dollars and, more important, your valuable time reading this book. I'll tell you right now: I have a great college education but not an MBA. I didn't interview salespeople in 15 countries to come up with the material for this book. What I have accomplished during the past 25 years is very successfully sell face to face on the street every day just like you! Frequently, those sales were more than $1 million each. For 10 of those 25 years, I have coached, mentored, and collaborated with 10 of my own salespeople and have trained many other salespeople and district managers. I've also attended most all of the national sales training programs. With that being said, I'm writing this book in hopes of helping you produce more results, become a better sales professional, and, more important, more fully enjoy the rewards of our profession. The themes in this book will be very simple and will be themes that you can incorporate in your day-to-day selling events, not themes or lists that sound good but are forgotten a day later. I will also frequently use metaphors from everyday life that relate to sales and the sales process because I believe we, as salespeople, learn differently from others. Sales can be very tough at times, and I don't know about you, but I've made my share of mistakes during the past 25 years, and I'd like to share some of them with you so you can avoid these mistakes. It's these same experiences and mistakes that will make this book profitable for us. By purchasing this book, we could spend time collaborating, sharing common ground, and becoming better at our profession, the sales profession. Always remember that it's your internal "yearning to learn" that will make you great in sales, as well as life itself!

One last thing: I don't know about you, but I'm tired of reading books on sales that are so serious. List after list, reminder after reminder, rule after rule—my book is different. You will learn many new concepts and will reinforce existing concepts by looking at them in a different light, but most of all, you will laugh and enjoy this book. You'll laugh just reading the chapter titles.

STREET SMART SELLING

SCOTT F. NIEDERMEYER

Full Court Press
Oconomowoc, Wisconson

Published by Full Court Press
4506 Deer Park Road
Oconomowoc, WI 53066

Publisher's Cataloging-in-Publication Data

Niedermeyer, Scott F.

Street smart selling. – Oconomowoc, WI : Full Court Press, 2006.

p. ; cm.

ISBN: 0-9772910-0-6

ISBN13: 978-0-9772910-0-7

1. Selling-Study and teaching. 2. Selling. 3. Sales management. I. Title.

HF5438.2 .N54 2005

658.85-dc22 2005936284

Book production and coordination by Jenkins Group, Inc.
www.bookpublishing.com

Interior design by 1106 Design

Cover design by Flight Path Creative

Printed in the United States of America

10 09 08 07 06 • 5 4 3 2 1

Dedication

This book is dedicated to Susan, my lovely, supportive wife of 25 years; my son, Ryan, a determined young man; and my parents, Fred and Annette Niedermeyer, for their relentless support and guidance. Last but not least, this book is also dedicated to all the clients who have trusted my solution or my sales team's solution versus many other solutions.

Contents

ACKNOWLEDGMENTS ix
ABOUT THE AUTHOR xi
INTRODUCTION xiii
ARE YOU A SALES PROFESSIONAL? xv

FACE-TO-FACE SELLING STRATEGIES 1
- The Art of the Sales Call 3
- Your Written Pre-Call Plan 5
- The Warm-Up Phase 10
- The "Meet" Thermometer 13
- Creating Aura 16
- The Information-Gathering Phase 19
- How Big Is Your Client's 10 Spot? 24
- Time of Possession 27
- Showtime, the Presentation 32
- Presentation Checklist 36
- Objection Handling 39
- A Time for Closure 43
- Information Overload 47
- Don't Drive off without Paying 49
- The Postgame Interview 52
- Keep Perceiving and Practicing 55

NON-FACE-TO-FACE SELLING STRATEGIES 57
- Strategically Speaking in Sales 59
- The Processing Agent 60
- The Inner Circle 63
- The Cart before the Horse 66
- Gone Fishing 70

- Pinball Wizard 75
- Expose the Scoreboard 79
- Win, Place, or Show 82
- It's Tied, and It's Overtime 85
- Waiting to Lose 87
- How Well Do You Wait? 89
- Self-Talk Radio 91
- Showboating in the End Zone 94
- Oscars for Your Supporting Cast 96
- Park Your Own Turbo 98

ORGANIZE AND SUCCEED 103
- The Tangled Underwear Award 105
- A Salesperson's Worst Nightmare 110
- Chinese Fire Drill 113
- Time-Out 115
- Top 75/Top 30 119
- The Black Box 125
- Driven, but Where Are You Driving? 128
- Shaken, not Stirred 133

A TIME TO MOVE ON 135
- It's Easier to Fail in Sales Than You Think 137
- How Many Sharks Swim in Your Tank? 140
- Flying above the Clouds 143
- Polishing Plan B 146
- The Writing Is on the Wall 148
- A Few Words about Résumés 151
- Off to Greener Pastures 155

Appendix—BEGINNING SALES MANAGEMENT 159
- The 5 C's of Sales Management 161
- The Candle and the Glass 166
- Joint Sales Calls 169
- Assessing Sales Talent 172

Acknowledgments

It's very tough to balance work and family as a sales professional. The nights away from home and returning late on the nights you are home along with the constant sacrifices a sales professional's family makes in order to foster success simply add up over 25 years. It takes a special type of spouse to accept all of the above, and in my life, her name is Susan Niedermeyer. Susan set aside her profession for my profession. She handled a portion of our lives, and together we have met all challenges. I couldn't have done it without her, and my success and happiness today are simply because of her.

I only hope my son, Ryan, goes into sales some day and this book helps in some small way. His life is ahead of him, and without him, I wouldn't laugh nearly as much as I do today.

I also attribute my success to my parents. Many core beliefs and values are molded at a very early age, and they did a great job. They instilled a need to be fair with people. They taught me how to be sensitive to and empathetic of others. They fostered a work ethic in me that has withstood the test of time. They planted the seeds of spiritual conviction at an early age. They made sure athletics and exercise were a permanent part of my life for the personal and physical rewards they bring to life. They instilled a goal-oriented nature in me and the wherewithal to realize the power of individual effort or embracing a team to reach those goals. They were always there to listen, support, and advise in a soft way. The way they handled their lives was a guiding light for the way I should handle my life. All of these experiences are in themselves great, but they become even greater when you try to instill them in your own children and realize how difficult they are to achieve in another person. I thank you, Mom and Dad, for everything.

Certainly my success was also a result of our "Super Bowl" sales team: Michelle Rice, Scott Slaughter, Brad Timmerman, Carl Canter, Dan Mahlik, Eric Halverson, Sandy Pochowski, Kelly Brazelton, Jamie Lewis, and Heidi Smith. Together, we ruled. We were one. Nothing stopped us. Our customers *were* king. We had fun, and we achieved many personal goals during those days. Our success together both personally and professionally and the shear power a great team can provide will always remain as the pinnacle of success in my sales career.

About the Author

Scott Niedermeyer has very successfully sold in the commercial furniture industry for 25 years. During the first 15 years, Scott sold face to face on the street and directly called on end users in the Fortune 500, health care, government, higher education, and architectural marketplaces and managed various distributors in those markets. For the past 10 years, he owned one of the largest sales organizations in the commercial furniture industry and mentored 10 sales representatives in three states. His company always performed in the top three of 27 districts, and three years out of 10, his firm ranked number one in performance. Yearly sales averaged $25–$30 million, and frequently, individual orders were well over the million-dollar mark. All this success was due to his great outside sales staff and his impeccable inside support staff. His company's strategies were always clear and simple to grasp and understand. Most of all, these strategies were always targeted toward surpassing mutually rewarding business and personal goals for all participants. Scott's "will to win" along with his sincere, empathetic nature have been the cornerstones for his success. This book represents the culmination of his passion for sales and the sales process.

Introduction

"Sales stars" are *organized, structured* selling machines. They *orchestrate* their selling events. They artfully probe their clients by asking the *best* questions, *patiently* listening, and correctly perceiving what was said *and* not said! Sales stars produce by gaining advances, not continuations, and their "will to win" creates the determination to *close* the sale. Sure, sales stars hunt for the order, but they follow up on everything after the sale till the customer is 100% happy with the end result. Sales stars *build* relationships over time, and they do it because they invest the time required in the first place, and then they are empathetic to their client or their inside support staff's needs and desires. Sales stars detail and chart their progress toward their company and personal goals *and* achieve most of them. Last but not least, sales stars *constantly* prospect for new clients by referral, research, and strategic targeting, and it's this ongoing prospecting plan that always keeps their funnel *and* their savings account full!

Is this *you*? Does this have *you* written all over it? The answer is: probably to an extent. Achieving the statements above is an ongoing effort in sales. The day you *think* you have arrived at achieving the statements above or have given up on trying to achieve the above is the day you will stunt your growth and potential in the sales profession and become complacent. The "yearning to learn" must always be present in sales. More important, this yearning to learn *must* transfer into execution in your daily life in sales. Salespeople who don't change and challenge themselves with new tacts and actually implement these changes level out in performance, both professionally and personally, and, yes, they become complacent. Each one of us has a degree of complacency in us. In sales, complacency eventually becomes the kiss of death. It takes mental and physical energy to ward off complacency. Sure, this book is about sales, but it's more about an effort to help *you* ward off complacency. If you implement one idea in this book as long as you are in sales, it will be worth it—worth it for you *and* for me! If this book helps you kick complacency in the butt, I'll be very happy. If this book helps you bring more money home to your family, I'll be very happy. If this book helps you become more of a "sales professional," I'll be very happy. We may never actually meet, but the reward for me for all the time I spent writing this book will be if I can help *you*! Not just for a couple days after you read this book but forever in *your* life in sales. If one of these concepts is truly one that you will *commit* to take with you forever in sales, I would like to hear from you because that would truly be a reward for me. E-mail me at scott@snaconsulting.net.

It's showtime!

Are You a Sales Professional?

Remember the days when we were back in grade school? At the beginning of the year, we usually had assigned seats, but in time, we got a chance to sit anywhere. I always sat toward the back of the class if given the chance, and maybe some of you know exactly why! Some people loved to sit in the front of the class. I was never very fond of those people. When the teacher would ask a question, their hands would fly into the air as if they were trying to pull stars out of the sky. And if that wasn't disturbing enough, then they would begin their verbal antics like, "Oh! Mrs. Smith! Oh! Oh! I know! I know! Please call on me!" During all that excitement, I would begin to look as busy as possible. I'd look for a pencil or open my desk lid—anything to seem too busy to answer the question. Most of you know what happened next. Through this sea of raised hands, the teacher would say, "Scott, what's the answer to the question?" Usually, I would come up with four answers in hopes that one of them would stick, but invariably my answers would be wrong. Then, the teacher would call on someone in the front of the class, all the other hands would lower, and the answer would flow eloquently out of one of the hand raiser's mouths. If that same scenario was presented today and the class was on "sales," would you be in the front of the class with me? I hope you and I would be up in front with our hands raised high—but *we* would stop short of offering any verbal antics, right?

True success in sales begins with an attitude. It's an attitude that sales *is* your profession, not the consolation prize in your career. It's **this proud attitude** about your profession that will help you survive through thick and thin. It's **this pride in your profession** that will carry you through the relentless prospecting, the continuous rejection, and the long drives back from that hard-to-reach client. It's your deep "will to succeed" in the sales profession that will carry you through the next sales slump or your sales manager's critique after a disappointing sales call together. It's your personal yearning to learn your profession by constantly reading books or attending seminars that will continually take you to new heights in the sales profession. *Take a moment and go to a quiet spot and reflect on all of this. Without this deep-down passion to be successful in sales, you will always be average, at best, and career frustration will dog you every step of the way.*

This great attitude will then begin to transform your actions. The next proposal you make will be more professional. You'll look at it and say, "No, it's not the best I can do. I've got the time, and I'll change it!" For the next sales event you encounter, you'll plan ahead of the call, conduct yourself more professionally in the call, and articulate yourself more succinctly. You will begin to create an aura around yourself and your actions. This aura will lead to an attention to detail in everything you do, including how you dress. You will begin to treat others with even greater respect, especially your support staff and fellow sales associates. This newfound sense of pride, attitude, passion, and professionalism will appear and will be a part of everything and everybody you touch.

The real test after you embrace this genuine pride in your profession, the sales profession, will be the next social setting you encounter. It will be tested when a new acquaintance asks you, "What do you do for a living?" Will you answer, "I'm in sales" or "I sell for a living" or "I sell for XYZ company" or "I work for XYZ company"? Think about it long and hard because you should reply, **"I truly have a passion for sales, and I love selling for XYZ company."**

Could we agree that you will take this great attitude and pride in your profession with you the rest of the way as you read this book because you and I are in the front of the class and we have a passion for sales?

FACE-TO-FACE SELLING STRATEGIES II

THE ART OF THE SALES CALL

We have all been on a great sales call. Nothing feels better than sitting in your car after a killer call. Everything went smoothly. You weren't as nervous as you thought you would be during the call. The customer was interested in what you were saying, and he didn't say, "Get out and stay out!" He said that you should call back in six months and that you should send some literature. You were able to tell him about most of your products, but you had wished you could have also mentioned just a few more products to see whether he had any interest in them. He seemed to really like you, and the two of you hit it off, so to speak. In fact, you both like to sail, so it's going to be a good account some day. It's only a matter of time before you win at this account.

We all know a great sales event could mean so much more than what is achieved above. ***In fact, what was achieved above?*** After reading the following chapters, you'll realize that not much of anything was achieved above! We will cover the key aspects of making great sales calls. Making a great sales call is an art form, and it usually begins with a written **pre-call plan**. Then, the **warm-up phase** is critical to achieving rapport and connection early in the call for the rest of the call. The **information-gathering phase** is so critical for value creation and desire development. "**Showtime**" is your chance to strategically throw your darts, hopefully at a target that you have created during the call. **Objection handling** is always an exciting phase. Last, but not least, there's all those theories at the end, usually called "**closing techniques.**" *Are you ready to rumble?*

YOUR WRITTEN PRE-CALL PLAN

It's Christmas Day. In a matter of minutes, your kids have ripped through the presents that took hours to wrap. They are off with their long-sought-after items and are as happy as can be, and it's just you and the unassembled gas grill your wife gave you. You open the box, lay out the pieces, and think for a second, maybe longer, that you could probably put this together without the instructions. You soon remember how much you hate rework and decide to open the bag with the instructions and get started. Your wife is in the kitchen and is getting ready for all those in-laws who are coming over in a matter of hours. One last item to make and at the same time she is wondering whether she remembers how to whip up those killer cookies from Martha Stewart for the kids. But, in the end, your wife reaches for the recipe book and reads the recipe rather than making a last-minute mistake.

Can *you* label a sales call "great" without following a written recipe for sales call success or a "**pre-call plan**"? I certainly could never consider a sales call truly great unless I sat down before the call and wrote down a strategy for the call. So many salespeople today seem to be totally comfortable winging it on sales calls. They venture into their calls and are armed with their brochures, proposals, or, in some cases, just themselves and a pen. They know exactly how the call will go: they will present their proposal, ask for any questions, and hope for an order, and if they are unsuccessful, then they will try to follow up at a later date. It's that simple; they have done it time and again. **To be a truly great salesperson on a truly great sales call, a written pre-call plan is a must!**

Almost every book on sales has a type of pre-call form in it. The actual form you decide to use is not important; what's important is that you decide to use a written plan with a specific format. Jotting several questions on your pad frantically before the call just doesn't work. Not only does it not work, but it also doesn't look professional. Take the time to embrace a format you enjoy, copy it, pad it with a three-hole punch, and keep it in your binder at all times so you are always ready to prepare for any call at any time.

The pre-call plan that I like to use is on the following pages. I've revised it several times, and for me it works great! Several key concepts are covered in the plan:

- **The Warm-Up Phase.** This is a very important phase of any sales event. Decide before you walk into the call what types of questions you will ask to warm up the sales call. This is not idle chitchat. It's planned, specific, and productive.
- **The Information-Gathering Phase.** The questions you decide to ask in this phase are also very important. Take the time before the call to decide on some very good questions, questions you will be proud that you asked when you get back in your car after the sales event.
- **Advances.** These sets of next steps, both primary and secondary, are critical to target at the end of the call. (1)
- **Explicit Needs.** These are the needs that are the client "got to haves" you uncover in the call. Hopefully, you are able to artfully probe and draw out many of these during the call.

- **Next Meeting Date and Time.** The best time to set the next meeting date and time between you and the client is when you are on the current call.
- **Notes.** This is simply an area for the various notes you take during the visit, and it is important to take notes—good notes!
- **Critique Section.** This area is for you to take a moment to evaluate your success on the different aspects of the call.

Even polished, seasoned sales professionals rely on written pre-call plans before they make their sales calls. They realize that the time they take prior to the call will pay for itself in spades during the call. This quiet pre-planning regiment allows them to remember to ask questions they might have otherwise forgotten to ask. They decide that this time they will ask "the question" they have always wanted to ask but never had time, forgot to ask in prior contacts, or didn't have the guts to ask until now. Or they just decide that they are going to look and act professional in the customer's eyes by referring to a document that shows pre-thought about how important their time is with that client.

---

(1) Neil Rackham, *Spin Selling*

■ Pre-Call Plan

Date: ______________________________

Contact: ______________________________

Company: ______________________________

Warm-Up Questions

1. ______________________________
   ____
   ____
2. ______________________________
   ____
   ____

Information-Gathering Questions

1. ______________________________
   ____
2. ______________________________
   ____
3. ______________________________
   ____
4. ______________________________
   ____
5. ______________________________
   ____
6. ______________________________
   ____

Advances:

Primary ______________________________

Secondary ______________________________

Explicit Needs Uncovered

____
____
____

Next Meeting Date ____________ **Time** _____

Scott Niedermeyer & Assoc. Phone: 262-560-1255

E-mail: *scott@snaconsulting.net*

Notes ____

____

____

____

____

____

____

____

____

____

____

____

____

____

____

____

____

____

____

____

Critique:

1. Talking percentage: (goal: 80% client, 20% rep)
   _____% client _____% rep
2. Sales call flow (1 to 5, 5 being the highest) ______________
3. Did I achieve the next logical advance? ________________
4. Did I have enough and the right support materials?______
5. Did I ask the questions I wrote down? _________________
6. Did I develop rapport? _____Did the client laugh?_______
7. Did I strike a common thread with the client? ___________
8. Did I develop a desire to continue with me?_____________
9. Areas for improvement________________________________

   ____

   ____

   ____

THE WARM-UP PHASE

You and your significant other have planned this getaway for some time now. You've planned a trip to a cabin in the north woods. No phones, no distractions—just the two of you and a warm fire for a couple of winter nights. You finally arrive after a long day at the office, then a tiring drive up north, and as the two of you are about to open the door to the chalet, the guests next door drive up in a car that looks very familiar. It gets closer, and you suddenly realize that it's a car you've seen at your accounts. Sure enough, you have seen it before! It's your archrival and his guest, **and they are staying right next door**! All the excitement over the weekend has been tossed out the window. You can't believe it. Your archrival is staying next door! Some kind of escape this will be! You begin to try to settle down and start to build a fire to take the chill out of the air in more ways than one. It's going to be cold tonight, 10 below zero. This fire better be a good one. You remember the days you spent in scouting: smaller pieces of wood, then larger ones, in the form of a teepee. You check the flue and even take the time to look up the chimney just to make sure you see sky. It's open all right. Nothing is going to ruin this evening—well, at least not the fire.

You light the fire, stand back, and hope for the best. Sure enough, it takes like it should, and you settle into the couch with your favorite drink. As you get up, you take one more look at the cabin next door, and that's when you notice someone standing on the deck. Who the heck would be standing on the deck on a winter night at 10 below zero? It's your archrival! You also notice all the windows are open and smoke is billowing out of the windows. You've been there before. Your archrival must have forgotten to open the flue, and you just laugh to yourself, wallow in satisfaction, raise your glass to toast him, and leisurely stroll past your blazing fire, casually throw on another log, and realize how thirsty you are again.

The **warm-up phase** of a sales call is very critical to your success on that call. Many books pass over this phase fairly quickly. I'm a big believer in the warm-up. As long as you are talking to a decision maker, I believe if the warm-up lasted the entire call, it wouldn't be all bad. Some say it's friendship, not salesmanship. The warm-up phase is all about friendship, rapport, connection, and common interests. It's also a time for salespeople to relax, settle down, and put any nervousness behind them. The warm-up is also a time to get the client talking. Sure, the questions you pre-planned are to be asked, but so is anything that appears as you walk into the account. Great salespeople keep their radar on high as soon as they walk in; they note anything that makes them curious about the situation. The epitome of a great warm-up is to laugh a little with the client. Just the chance to share something fun together will go a long way to help make that call great. The warm-up is all about the beginnings of developing or continuing trust between the two of you. It's just like building a great fire on a cold night. Let **the client** signal when the warm-up is over. A quick look at the time, a "Well, we better get going," or just the calming down of a phase well executed is the signal. Pick up on it as soon as it appears, and move on. The warm-up has officially ended. Hopefully, the client is talking, you're relaxed, and the fire between you is hot!

Remember, the warm-up is a very legitimate phase. Salespeople can't wait to talk about their stuff, and they tend to blow by this phase as if it were just meaningless chitchat. Great salespeople know they are going nowhere unless the event is warmed up at the beginning. In their eyes, the warm-up means developing a true connection and interest in the client, not anything fake just to get an order. They understand that this trust is what will eventually get them the initial order and subsequent orders. More important, when the chips are down later in the relationship, it's the time they spent developing rapport and trust that will pay dividends later in the relationship.

Some phrases that might help you develop questions for the warm-up are as follows:

- Before we start, I've always wondered why _____.
- I'm curious; would you by any chance know so-and-so?
- I couldn't help but notice on my way in today _____.
- I've seen _____ as I travel and I've always wondered _____.
- Has the recent _____ affected your company?
- How was your weekend? Did your child's team win? How was your wife's trip? So, tell me about your vacation.
- Your office is beautiful. I like _____. What a view! It's so organized.
- Looks like you enjoy _____.
- Tell me about _____.
- Have you ever been able to _____?
- Now that had to be an experience! Tell me about it.
- I have to ask: what's the significance behind _____?
- There must be a story associated with _____.

THE "MEET" THERMOMETER

We all are familiar with the meat thermometer and its role in gauging whether a selection of meat is cooked to perfection. The thermometer is placed in the meat, and the needle rises quickly until it reaches temperature. Certainly it's important to make sure the thermometer doesn't stick through the meat so a false reading is received—a false reading that is *higher* than the true state of the situation.

Do salespeople at times have false readings as to the warmth they achieved on their sales calls? Is their impression of how well they connected with a client different from how the client feels about the same event? So many times I have heard, "We hit it off great! We both like fishing!" or "My cousin knows his brother-in-law!" or "You won't believe it, but our kids went to the same college!" All that is great, but some salespeople start to believe that those remote commonalities will propel them to the order stage easier than normal. Those ties might break a "tie," but the salesperson still has to accomplish a great deal to get the game tied, and he or she should focus on those issues more than anything else. Also remember that "meat" only stays hot while there is a good fire nearby. The minute the salesperson leaves the client's office, the cooling-off process begins. It takes constant follow-up to keep the situation hot. The best salespeople create ways to stay in touch with their contacts and realize that the longer they are away, so are the chances of getting any orders.

Correctly perceiving warmth, connection, or rapport developed in a sales event or a series of sales events is paramount. If the two of you had a "meet thermometer" and compared the temperatures that each of you achieved in your recent sales event together, would the temperatures truly be close? Or would your meet thermometer read hotter than your client's? Remember the time you were about to purchase an automobile from one dealership but visited the less favored dealership one last time? Were you nice to the salesperson? Did you seem warm to that salesperson even though the salesperson at the soon-to-win dealership was your favorite? Did you give the losing salesperson any indication you were about to purchase from his or her competition later that day? Probably not! The point in all of this is to be very critical of the warmth you perceive in a sales event. It's time to bring out your devil's advocate, check yourself out, and be realistic about the warmth you actually created. Just remember to tone it down a little because more times than not, *your* reading on the meet thermometer is higher than your client's. But don't stop or temper any of your tactics because of it until the order is well in hand. Then and only then can you relax and truly discuss fishing together.

If you do encounter a sense of cooling in the relationship during your next visit, those perceptions are usually right! It's time to ask a few questions:

- You seem cooler on our solution today. Have you possibly become more interested in another solution?
- Could we spend a moment talking about what has happened since we met last?
- The last time we met, it seemed like you were very interested in our _____. I sense something has changed since then.

It's this sixth sense and your ability to probe around these perceptions that will propel you in the sales profession. More important, however, is your ability to get the situation back in your court or realize you are too far behind in the race to catch up by the finish line.

Keep your fires hot!

CREATING AURA

Have you ever wondered what clients say about you after you have left the sales call? Do they go back to their office and are they happy about the interaction and the value it created? Did they compare you with their favorite supplier, and did you just reinforce why they use that supplier instead of you? Did they have a particular need they didn't tell you about because you didn't ask? Or did they have a particular need they didn't tell you about because they didn't want you to come back? Did you fail their tests of you during the interview? Did you get into your car and think about how wonderful the encounter went, and clients are thinking about how they couldn't wait for you to leave?

It's important for salespeople to continue to try to create an "aura" with their clients. In the early phases of a sales career, it's tough to even think of your aura, much less be able to create one. However, as confidence grows, so does the ability to begin to create an aura on sales calls with the customer. Keys to aura creation:

- **Dress professionally.** Take concern in the way you appear. It makes a big difference in the way you are perceived.

- **Keep your mannerisms in check.** Many times we are not fully aware of how certain mannerisms affect people around us. On a joint sales call with your sales manager, have your manager look for any of your mannerisms that might make your client uncomfortable. Work on those mannerisms and eliminate them.
- **Embrace your pre-call plan.** The pre-call plan can have a large effect on the aura you create in a sales call just by being more relaxed because you planned ahead for that call. Use the warm-up phase to do exactly that: warm up the call not only for yourself but also for your client.
- **Perceive anxiety.** Be on the lookout for anxiety when it begins to develop. Perceive any disconnect with your clients and the anxiety that may follow. Remember that your client holds the key to doing business with him or her. Some salespeople are oblivious to any anxiety that appears in a call because they are so focused on their product or solutions. Perceiving anxiety as soon as it appears—and probing on it immediately—is very important.
- **Talk in everyday language.** Some salespeople think they will impress the client with all sorts of industry jargon. Actually, that jargon has the reverse effect; it creates a disconnect between the salesperson and client and doesn't impress anyone. Talk in simple terms so everyone stays on the same page—the client's page.
- **Be true to your word.** Accomplish what you promise to accomplish when you say you will accomplish it! Never promise anything you can't accomplish. Always tell the whole truth and nothing but the truth!
- **Be positive.** Salespeople with auras are positive, always believing in the value they can create for the client. They believe they are the best at what they do and that the client would be best served by using them, and if not, these salespeople lead

that client in the best direction regardless of what they actually sell.

- **Product knowledge.** The salespeople with the best auras know their products the best. They study their products whenever they have time, or else they make time! They are truly a resource for their customers and a consultant on their needs and related solutions.
- **Seek advice.** Salespeople with auras seek advice because they always want to know what others are thinking and how to continually conduct themselves better. They are an open book, and they ask their clients how they are doing so they get constant feedback as to the track they are on and how close to the target they are getting.
- **Articulate professionally.** Salespeople with the biggest auras select their words well and are professional about doing so. They never downgrade the competition. They may point out differences, but they never pass judgment on the client.

Remember: this aura is defined by the clients, not the salespeople. The clients are the judges of this aura. These salespeople are not self-centered; they are centered on the clients! It's the clients' opinions that count. It's the clients' perceptions of the salespeople that count, not the salespeople's perceptions of themselves!

THE INFORMATION-GATHERING PHASE

If we've decided that the warm-up phase is important, wait till we strategize on this next phase: the information-gathering phase. So many concepts are all balled up in this phase that it's tough to even call it "information gathering," but it's a broad enough term that it's probably most appropriate.

What I have found over the years is that many salespeople realize they are supposed to ask questions and uncover needs, wants, and desires and all of that, but when it comes to actually doing it, they have a very difficult time. Sometimes it's because they simply can't come up with any questions that seem appropriate. Sometimes they have asked some questions and they feel that's enough of that and it's time they strut their stuff, finally. Sometimes the questions they decide to ask lead them off in a tangent or tangents and they get so far away from the main event that they have a difficult time getting back on track. It's important to remember that this phase is specifically designed to find out whether you're talking to a prospect. Not everyone you talk to is going to need, much less actually use, your solutions. In fact, some books have said that you will win one-third of your opportunities and lose one-third of your opportunities, and it's what you do on the last third that will make you great. (2) **I honestly believe that in the information-gathering phase, salespeople should simply focus on questions about the client's current situation, whether there is any desire *in the client's eyes* to change the current situation in any way in the future, and if so, whether the client desires to describe an ideal picture of the future and what current frustrations it could eliminate, who would paint this picture, and do they desire *you* to help paint it with them for a cost that is acceptable?** Wow, that's a heck of a sentence: eighty-three words, six commas, seven concepts. However, it's the essence of the information-gathering phase if not the entire sales process!

We have to begin by asking questions about their current situation. I call it "target development." Salespeople quite honestly have a number of "darts" (solutions) to throw in a sales call. It could be a new distribution center, a new product, new features or benefits for an existing product, a state-of-the-art customer service center, new marketing jargon, or 100 years of being in business. Whatever the darts, salespeople love to throw them. Some of these darts over the years have been truly lucky darts, darts that have won orders! Some darts just look pretty, and salespeople like throwing them not because they ever win orders with them but because they just look good. Some darts sound great when they travel through the air; they have a certain whisper to them for some reason. Some darts are simply duds; they haven't worked for years, but they are still in the bag, so why not throw them? **It's not so much about the darts or solutions; it's more about the target.** Salespeople like to throw these darts before they know where the target is specifically, much less the 10 spot on the target. Salespeople should place all their darts in a bag and set the bag well out of reach for a while, and then they should ask good questions and find the client's target. Better yet, they should ask such great questions that they actually find the 10 spot on the client's target! Let's look for the target together.

Current Situation Questions:

- I certainly enjoyed talking about _____. I've never thought it was that funny. I'm wondering whether we could talk about *how* you handle _____?
- *What* happens *when* _____?
- *Who* gets involved if _____?
- I'm curious as to *why* the situation would change when _____.
- I suppose that if that happened, then it would affect ___.
- Does _____ ever become a frustration?
- Tell me whether you have ever tried to _____.
- Why didn't it work?

Great salespeople ask these questions to catch up and because they are genuinely intrigued by the client's current situation. They don't live, eat, and sleep that client's situation every day of every week. Quite honestly, it's simply a time to *begin* to understand whether that salesperson can help. It's a time to begin to formulate an opinion of whether this account is a dud or an actual prospect. The important word in the sentence above is the word "begin." The ability to formulate a correct opinion, or what I like to say is the correct perception, of the potential value of the account is critical. I believe salespeople who don't produce as much as other salespeople do so to a degree because they don't perceive the value in a particular account that another salesperson might perceive. Or they perceive potential value that really isn't there over time. Or they don't have the sales ability to develop the potential value that they honestly perceive. Without a clear, correct perception about the client's current situation, the possible potential of an account will never materialize.

With the client's current situation well in hand, it's time to envision the future. It's time to get out the crystal ball and the tarot cards and become "Karnack"—or in simpler terms get out a new piece of canvas and begin to paint a picture of the future.

Desire to Change the Future Questions:

- Thanks for helping me catch up on life at XYZ company; it sounds exciting to say the least. Is there anything you would like to change in the future if you could?
- Is there always something that has loomed important but the company has never had the chance to actually accomplish?
- As the events in the future unfold, what, in your opinion, will the company have to embrace now in order to prepare?
- As you look out into the future, is there one concept that you would like to tackle first?
- If you were me, someone who is focused on making the future brighter, where would you start at this account?
- Tell me whether I'm being too bold, but after what I've heard so far, it seems to me that it would be great if _____, and if we could _____, that would be even more beneficial!
- Let's talk about budget for a moment. How would you budget for the funds to actually change and prepare for the future like we talked about today?
- After the time we have spent together so far, would there be any reason why XYZ company wouldn't consider our solutions if deemed valuable?
- Let's say I could make the future brighter. Who would be involved in deciding on the parameters, timetable, and associated costs?

All of the questions in this arena are categorized as "desire development" questions. Is there a desire to change the current situation? Is there a desire to prepare now for the future? Is there a desire to add something to what the customer presently does now so as to make things better in the future? Has their current situation created such a desire to change that finally, enough is now enough and it's time to change? It's very important that salespeople don't *create* this desire for their client in an effort to sell their solutions. Great salespeople find accounts with genuine desire and pursue them like a piranha. If the contact they are currently calling on doesn't seem to have any desire and they know desire should exist under the circumstances, they search out other people in the organization like a heat-seeking missile zeroed in on the desire they know has to be present somewhere at the account. I'll mention the word "persistent" at this point in time. Is a piranha persistent? Is a heat-seeking missile persistent? You bet—and so are great salespeople! When they smell blood or perceive heat, they are all over it!

> *It's time to ask yourself whether the* ***information-gathering phase*** *has uncovered a genuine target at this account. By artful questioning, have you taken the cover off the target in the client's eyes and exposed the 10 spot? Have you uncovered strong desire to actually change the future in the eyes of the client? And last, but not least, do you have any darts or solutions that could hit that client's 10 spot, and if so,* ***which specific darts or solutions are you going to throw, and has your questioning uncovered why these particular solutions seem most appropriate?***

(2) Steve Schiffman, *Telesales*

HOW BIG IS YOUR CLIENT'S 10 SPOT?

Most everyone is familiar with the target shown below. Whether you are a hunter, enjoy a game of darts, or have tried your luck at a county fair over the years, the closer you hit to the center, the more points you score! It's obvious why the center is so small—because it makes it tough to get a 10 and hence, the challenge.

All salespeople like to work with a different target similar to the one shown on the next page. Now that's a target! How about that 10 spot! Anybody want to play a game of darts? I'll bring the target!

How do salespeople develop accounts or sales strategies that enlarge the 10 spot like the target shown on the next page so they win more often? Hopefully, this book will help you answer this intriguing question to a greater extent. For now, let's just focus on asking some questions that would begin to enlarge the 10 spots on your current sales opportunities. These series of questions might just set you apart from the rest of the pack, or these questions might help you understand where you stand at any given time in the sales process so you can evaluate how large your 10 spots are currently.

- What place do you think I'm in right now? I know you are considering several solutions, and I'm just wondering where we stand at this point in time and whether we can get in first place by the finish line.
- What do you like about the competition that differentiates them?
- In your opinion, what could I do or offer to help me get into first place?
- I sense something has changed since our last meeting. You seem a little cooler on our proposal. Are my feelings off base?
- I get the feeling that it's pretty much of a tie right now. What could I do to break the tie and be given a chance to prove myself?
- I feel as though I'm in pretty good shape on this part of the sale, but I feel very vulnerable on this part. What are your thoughts?
- I get the feeling I'm too far behind to catch up by the finish line. Are my perceptions correct?
- I'm going to take a shot at the way I see this one coming down. I think XYZ will get _____ and ABC will receive _____, and I don't mean to be bold, but I think we will receive _____. So, how far off am I?

- What could I do to take this one off the table right now?
- If I offered _____, would we have a deal?
- I was able to get approval on _____ and on _____, but I can give only this much on _____. Can we move forward together?
- I honestly can't perform by the date you desire unless we decide this week. I'm sorry. Maybe my competition can still perform, but I can't, and I don't want to let you down after all the time we have spent and trust we've created between us.

Increasing your chances of winning sales opportunities is all important. Hopefully, these questions will begin to help the process. You certainly won't always score a 10, even when you've developed a larger than normal 10 spot. But, use these questions *and* develop others so you always know where the 10 spot is and how big it is, and never stop trying to make it bigger!

TIME OF POSSESSION

There is a concept in football called "time of possession." This is an analysis of the amount of time each team controls or is able to possess the football. Obviously, if you have the ball, you can score. Salespeople like "holding the ball." "Holding the ball" in sales equates to talking. Salespeople love to talk, and when they are talking, they believe they have their best chance to score points. Great football teams realize that they must possess the football to score points and win the game. However, if they execute well when they possess the ball and maximize their time of possession, they can still win even though they may possess the ball a fewer number of minutes than their competition.

The same is true in sales. The best salespeople are not the ones who talk the most. Success in sales and talking percentage are related but not in the way you might think. I believe the best salespeople actually talk the least. They execute so well when they have "the ball" or when they are talking that they run circles around salespeople who talk a great deal and truly say very little. The 80/20 rule applies here as it does so many times. The best salespeople listen 80% of the time and talk 20% of the time as a rule. Certainly this percentage changes depending on what phase of the call is at hand, yet when the percentages add up at the end of the call, 80% listening and 20% talking are the case more times than not for the best salespeople.

There is an art to getting the client to talk 80% of the time in a call. It's not easy, especially for an inexperienced salesperson. Many books talk about open-ended questions at this point in time. We all know that an open-ended question is a question that evokes a response that has more than the word "yes" or "no." Open-ended questions are vital, but it's more than just asking open-ended questions. The best salespeople ask pre-planned questions that are intriguing for the client. They really get them thinking and talking, and better yet, their questions expose problems. Sometimes these problems become more obvious to the artful salesperson than to the client at the time. The best salespeople refrain from throwing one of their darts or solutions at this point and actually begin to more fully expose the problem itself and continue to blow up the problem in the customer's eyes. It's almost like the beginning stages of blowing up a balloon. It's tough to start blowing up a balloon, not unlike uncovering a problem in a sales call. But once the problem is exposed, the balloon becomes easier to blow up, as are the consequences that relate to the original problem. The next time you are on a sales call and you have uncovered a legitimate problem in the customer's eyes, blow it up with some additional or what I call "extender" questions. Blow that balloon up to the point it's about ready to pop, tie off the end of the balloon or problem, and go on to find the next problem. Don't throw one of your darts at it! The best salespeople artfully have blown up several balloons during the information-gathering phase, and they just leave them until the presentation phase of the call, or what I like to call "showtime." It's fascinating to watch these artful salespeople carefully choose their darts or solutions and take aim at the nice, fat balloons they have exposed. Then they take their time of possession during showtime and pop balloons like they are at a carnival, and their commission dollars just flutter to the ground!

Understanding that every industry has its different problem-exposing questions, the best salespeople begin to develop a list of questions that work. Certainly these questions don't work in all of their sales events all the time, but they keep track of them, they write them down, and they keep them in their binder for reference so they don't have to reinvent them all the time. In fact, as this list develops not only from their own experiences but also their peers' experiences, it becomes a very powerful list and one that is referred to before more and more of their sales calls as they develop the information-gathering questions on their pre-call plans. These salespeople also begin to master the art of the extender questions. Typical extender questions may begin as follows:

- That's interesting. Why would you say that?
- Is there anything else that makes you feel that way?
- What else tends to bother you about that situation?
- After hearing that, I'm just curious; are you also concerned about _____?
- Who else feels the same way you do about this?
- I bet that problem really affects _____.
- I can imagine that was a tough situation. Then what happened?
- Now that you mentioned it, I've often wondered why _____.
- I suppose having this problem affects your _____.
- I'll go out on a limb here, but I'm sure you also have this problem _____.

These extender questions keep the time of possession in the client's hands. Great salespeople are really curious not just for curiosity's sake; they truly are curious about everything because it's this information that will affect their ability to execute when they finally get a chance at "the ball." Believe it or not, it may take several sales calls before an artful salesperson actually "executes" (proposes, presents, etc.), and usually, when it is showtime and they finally get the ball, points are scored very quickly.

As listening becomes more and more of a salesperson's daily routine, it's important for the salesperson to become better and better at listening skills at the same time. Efficient listening takes time and practice. To listen efficiently, you first have to be interested in what's being said. If your questioning has led the client off on a tangent that is not of interest to what you sell, graciously bring the client back to something that interests you as it relates to your solutions solving his or her problems. It's also hard to listen well when you're thinking about something else, like the next question you are going to ask! Hopefully, you have the next question written down on your pre-call plan, so forget about it! Refer to it when it's time. Right now it's time to concentrate on how good the question you just asked is as it relates to the client's problems and your solutions. If it's a good question, throw in several extender questions to get more out of it. Always remember that if you've hit a "hot button," exploit it; don't move on till you've exposed all of it and blown it up. I'm always amazed how salespeople when they are on a hot target or problem decide to move on to another potential target. Does a heat-seeking missile move on to another target once it's on track? Seldom!

I like to use the analogy of the game Battleship. We've all played Battleship either as a kid or with our kids. When the word "hit" has been stated, do you move on to another area of the board? Heck no! You start to exploit that area until you sink the battleship. Same in sales: if you have found a "hit" (hot button or problem) and it's something you may have a solution for, then stay at it until it's fully exposed. But remember that it takes more than sinking one battleship to win the game. Look for the other ships on the board. They are out there! Find them. Also remember to save your solutions until you have found all the ships, not just the first ship. Your solutions will have a far greater impact if you offer them after you have first found all the ships (problems) on the board. Happy sailing!

SHOWTIME, THE PRESENTATION

You've "warmed up" the call, and the fire is hot! You've gathered information about the client's current situation and what he or she desires to change about the future. You have been able to artfully find problems and blow them up to the point where they are about to burst. You get the impression that at least at this point in time, the client desires for *you* to continue and offer some help. Now, finally, it's time to throw your darts. So, regardless of what has just been said over the past half hour or several sales calls, you finally get to start your pitch. You've practiced it so often, and it's a good day. You feel good, and this time the pitch should be one of your best. After a few moments, suddenly the pitch isn't going so well. You begin to second-guess what you're saying for the first time in your career. In the past, it all flowed out so perfectly, and now—well—you feel out of sorts. Are you losing it? Is this what the end feels like? You begin to realize, as you're throwing the second dart, that after all you've heard, most likely this client could care less about dart number 2! It's dart number 6 that would make the most sense. You begin to talk about dart number 6, and it all begins to make sense. This isn't the end; it's the beginning! It's the beginning of a lucrative career in the sales profession. Selectively choosing the darts you decide to throw based on the information gathered is the beginning of your real development in sales. You remember the days of talking about things the customer could have cared less about. The days where *you* spent time creating a need for a particular dart in the client's eyes only to have it backfire in the end because it really wasn't what he or she wanted in the first place. I'll make another bold statement that goes against most sales jargon. Salespeople don't create value; customers do! Customers take information from salespeople and create value based on that information. Value is in the eye of the beholder, and the client is the beholder. When the tables are reversed and you're out shopping, personally, you create value, right? You take all the information, look at all the materials, and hear all the pitches, and then you take the most valuable solution in your opinion, right? Sometimes you take the lowest price, and sometimes you don't. You purchase the solution because it holds the most value to you based on the price *and* all the other information received.

Now that we've decided that you don't have to throw **all** your darts, **slow down**! There's plenty of time now to spend some real quality time on the darts you do decide to throw based on the information you have received. Some salespeople talk so fast when they are presenting, and then, to make matters worse, they begin to use all their industry jargon in an effort to seem more impressive. There is only one problem: the customer was simply left in the dust 100 words ago. Less *is* more when it comes to the number of words required to make a point. Great salespeople artfully make their points with amazingly few words. They also seem so relaxed about it. They realize that they don't always have to say everything they have to say! Either they decide they have made their point and they simply decide not to say any more even though they could or they will save this additional information for later, when it's a better time. True professionals choose their words very artfully.

Silence is golden. Salespeople for some odd reason always feel as though someone has to be talking all the time. If nobody is talking, then time is a-wasting. It's almost like sitting in a cab in a traffic jam with the meter running. Create silence, cherish it, savor it, and regard it as special every time you *hear* it. Don't always be the one to break the silence either; let it just hang out there, cherish every second, and be amused by it. Oftentimes it gives the customer a chance to think or digest what's been said—which is exactly what you want to create. Certainly, we are not talking about the silence that is created by not knowing what to say. It's the silence that is created by knowing what to say next but deciding not to say it at all or just not yet.

The best presentations are simply the ones that create an environment where the customer is talking among himself or herself, brainstorming on how to make your solution work in his or her environment. Now that's talking! The **customer is king,** so let the king(s) speak. Audience interaction—involvement—is the epitome of a great presentation. There's that 80/20 rule working again.

It's also important in a group presentation to **find Waldo**, the decision maker. So often in group presentations, the key decision maker(s) are in the room. If you've done your homework, you know who they are before they arrive, or better yet, you have a relationship with them already. Sometimes it's a new group, and maybe it's best to begin your presentation by going around the room and finding out where everyone's area of interest lies and what they hope you will accomplish in the presentation. Most likely, by taking this "go around the room" tact, you'll find the Waldo(s). Maybe as important is the ability to find your **coach**. Always decide on your coach at the account, the one who will help you in a variety of ways after the presentation is over. The coach's importance is paramount.

Never over-promise, never! Say you'll check and that you don't know for sure. Say that you just want to make sure. Remember: you're selling trust along with a number of other things. Any let-down here will haunt you for the rest of the relationship. Be honest; check and make sure what you say you can do you can fully do. I remember a time when I was asked whether I could do something, and I busted my tail to find out. It took a great deal of time to check it out. But in the end, I could make it happen, and I called the client back and told him we could do what he was asking, and he said, "OK, I just wanted to know. Thank you." That was it. He just wanted to know! After all the time I spent on it, he just wanted to know! Now, I say, "I'll check to see whether we can do that, but why would you like it that particular way?"

If you have found problems that are truly important to the client, blown them up as big as you can, created the desire to let you *solve their problems with* your *solutions, then show-time will be like picking low-hanging fruit or popping balloons at a county fair with the specific darts you choose from five feet away! That is, until the client objects to what you are proposing!*

PRESENTATION CHECKLIST

You'll find very few lists in this book. After all the sales books you and I have read over the years, we must have read more than 100 lists of things we should do to be great at sales. Where are all of those lists today? Who knows! I believe in concepts, analogies, and associations to everyday life that we can relate to as we learn. If you want to skip past this chapter, please do so. Or if you believe it's valuable, then copy it and place it in your binder for reference.

The Do's and Don'ts of Presentations

- Be ahead of time! Be ahead of time! Be ahead of time! Get the point?
- Practice, practice, practice your presentations. Anybody got a mirror?
- Respond to questions with clear, focused responses in a calm, calculated demeanor.
- Ask good, pertinent questions, not questions for questions' sake.

- Always make sure everything works: your demo, your AV, the room, everything.
- Silence is golden! Refrain from always filling up the void.
- Always bring supporting literature for everyone at the party.
- Always be aware of time limits and never run past them.
- Always bring a pad of paper and take notes.
- Always start by going around the room and asking for clarification on what the client is expecting at the event and whether he or she has any questions or requests before you start or use the answers to these questions *as* your starting point.
- Never over-promise, never. Always say you'll check if you don't know **and do check**!
- Always **remember** names. **Write them down** and focus on them more than anything else at the beginning of the party and throughout the party.
- Know your audience ahead, during, and after. Find the deciding agent(s) or Waldo(s) and find your coach.
- Always stimulate audience involvement; the best parties are when everyone gets to talk, at any time, *and* where everyone does actually talk!
- Always be courteous, gracious, respectful, and non-judgmental—like you're running for office.
- Friends buy from friends; can you befriend them during the party?
- Always get a next step, one with a time line that everyone agrees to and one that involves the participants taking some action themselves, not just you taking all the action.

- **Perceive** who is on your side, which people you've lost, and who is really connecting with you and who isn't, and confirm it with someone afterward—ideally your coach!
- Any more? Break a leg!

OBJECTION HANDLING

"Objection, your Honor, objection! Your price is too high!"

"I'm not surprised my price is high. It's usually high because of our new state-of-the-art distribution center. Most times my cost is higher because of the costs associated with this new selling advantage I have over the competition. Your orders will flow through this center flawlessly, and you will receive exactly what you ordered with 99% accuracy time and time again. My competition doesn't have anywhere near this type of efficiency or the capacity to handle your varied ordering cycles."

"I'm high? There's no way I could be high! There must be something wrong. I'm never high. Maybe you looked at our proposal wrong or my competition made a mistake or we're not comparing apples and apples. Something is wrong. We are never high!"

"We're high? Well, I know I can knock another 5% off the price right now on the spot. Does that get us closer? Well, I know it would get us closer, but is it enough to get the order? Usually, if I have a chance to talk to my sales manager about it, I can get even another 5% off. Will 10% be enough to get the order?"

Objections, they can be exciting, can't they? How dare the customer question what we're trying to present or sell! Doesn't the customer know that lots of people have spent a great deal of time researching exactly what he or she needs and what he or she should purchase as it relates to this stuff? We think, eat, and sleep this stuff! We know what is best for the client and what price he or she should pay based on all sorts of research. We'll tell the client, and we'll put the client back in line—because we know what's best for the client. He or she will see when it's all said and done that what we are presenting is the best solution and price!

I would like for you to consider a simple path that might work as it relates to handling objections. Maybe you already implement this process subconsciously, but I just wanted to formalize a sequence that might either confirm how you handle objections or modify your present handling of objections.

Show empathy. "I feel bad our price is high. Quite honestly, I didn't know where we would actually price out, but it sounds like we're high. After all the time we have spent on this proposal, I know my being high has certainly not made our job any easier." Right out of the blocks, I believe we should empathize with the client's concerns. Empathy is described as "feeling someone else's pain" but not "putting yourself in someone else's shoes," which is labeled as sympathy. I really believe a quick casting aside of someone's pain is a mistake. A quick response or solution to someone's pain because we have been there so many times before is also a mistake. It might be the one-hundredth time you have heard this objection, which is another problem, but it's important to treat it like the first time you've heard the objection. "I can understand how you might feel that way. Is the only objection to our proposal based on price? Or are there other issues as well?"

Embrace and engage. "Could we take a moment to help me understand why you feel the way you do about _____?" Take some time to **embrace** the client's concerns, and treat the client as important because he or she is very important. Objections always have the potential to be the deal breaker or just the tip of a large iceberg. Stop and listen and absorb the client's feelings not only on the subject at hand but also if it relates to a much larger subject that is hidden under this one. "I appreciate the chance to hear about how you feel about _____. Could we talk about possible solutions you might consider acceptable?" Begin to **engage** the customer in the solution process. Sometimes you'll be surprised at how easy it is to solve the problem in the customer's eyes. It's important to let the customer be a part of the solution process because solutions you develop together achieve buy-in from the customer and truly become solutions.

Exploit. Certainly exploit a solution together on the customer's turf to begin the process, but I believe in many cases, it's best to then walk away, exploit more on your own, and think more fully about all the possible solutions and use this opportunity to set up another time to meet after you have had a chance to craft your best solution. Use this time away from the client to exploit away with everyone you deem appropriate to help you put this obstacle behind you and most important, behind the customer.

Extinguish. Present your solutions and extinguish the objection. Many salespeople feel they have extinguished an objection when in actuality it becomes one of the reasons for a lost sale down the road. It's important to remember that you must confirm that the objection is really extinguished in the customer's eyes, not just in your eyes. Make sure you spend the time to confirm that the objection is **truly** behind the two of you. Or if you can't solve it totally, make sure you have truly been able to offset it with other items. Words can be cheap at this point in time. Great salespeople use exacting perception and their customer's verbal confirmation that the objection is truly history.

Enter. Oftentimes, objections can appear late in the selling process. If they are truly handled, then it is time to ask for the order. "We've spent a great deal of time analyzing this proposal. It makes sense to me, and it seems like it makes sense to you. Let's move forward so we can secure _____." Either another objection appears and the process starts over again or it might be time to embrace a win! Also remember that a win is only the beginning, not the end!

Handle away! And the best of luck! You'll do great!

> *Remember when we were young and we blew up a balloon and then let the air out? Sometimes we would let the air out all of a sudden and the balloon would shoot across the room. Other times we held the end of the balloon with two hands and let the air out ever so slowly. Let the air out of your client's objections ever so slowly, and don't stop until the air is all gone!*

A TIME FOR CLOSURE

June begins the day and says to Ward, "Honey, can you fix the screen door this weekend?" "What's wrong with the screen door, dear?" Ward replies. "It closes so quickly I hardly get out of the door and it's slamming me on the—" June says in her special way. "Say no more dear. I get the picture. I'll look at it this weekend, dear. Is there anything else you would like me to fix this weekend?" says Ward. June says, "No, honey, not right now. Maybe I'll think of something later." "You probably will, dear," Ward says and smiles as he walks away.

Great salespeople close like a well-adjusted screen door. They are smooth, calculating, and consistent. They finish softly and quietly under control. Their closes are certainly not abrupt, quick, out of control, or unorganized. In fact, their goal has been throughout the entire process to have this phase become a natural conclusion to a well-orchestrated series of sales events.

Entire books have been written on closing techniques. Each industry embraces a different strategy on closing. No matter which closing technique your present sales job embraces, it's important to purchase one of the many books on closing and read it! All salespeople must close the sale in one way or another or they are not in sales—they are in "visiting." It's not important what technique you decide on using or whether you have your own set of techniques. **What matters is that you are comfortable using them, that they are natural for you, and, well, that they work!** If you've set up the situation properly in past visits and truly extinguished any objections, closing is just a natural conclusion for the customer. He or she has simply placed a higher value on and trust in *you* and *your* solution versus all the other solutions considered throughout the process. On the contrary, if the salesperson hasn't handled previous visits or objections well, then closing will be a difficult, uneasy event. Some books teach the "ABC" technique, which describes the concept of "always be closing." I don't embrace this. Just like a well-adjusted screen door, it takes time to get to the close, perceive the process, and decide when it's time to ask for the order—just like the last stage of a screen door closing, a nice soft latching at the end of a very smooth process.

Not all sales calls end by obtaining a commitment to order. Many sales calls end by receiving an "advance" of some sort. It's very important that a salesperson prepare *before* the actual sales call the type of next step or advance he or she ideally would like to achieve. This is called a "primary advance." At the same time, it's important to decide on a "fallback advance" or "secondary advance" just in case the primary advance isn't obtained. **A true advance is when a salesperson obtains the type of commitment that the customer will take an immediate, physical action or a step in some way or another that moves the process along in a specific direction that relates to getting an order.** Many times salespeople obtain advances that really don't move the process toward closure. These salespeople are just happy with getting next steps but fail to be honest with themselves about whether these next steps will actually add up to getting an order. Great salespeople are always getting their customers to advance with them in the process, and their advances have direction and rationale as they relate to winning the order. They create in their clients a desire to continue because as soon as these clients lose the desire to continue, these great salespeople realize their sale is as good as over!

Maybe at times in your life you've had a devil's advocate—a person who is always second-guessing your strategy or who offers a different viewpoint because he or she is more removed from the situation than you are at the present time. Can you be your own devil's advocate? Even though you're close to the situation, can you still shoot holes in your own plan? I believe that great salespeople play the role of devil's advocate for themselves all the time. They are hard on themselves. They actually second-guess themselves on their own strategies. They talk to themselves: "Oh, sure, Scott. You just try to convince yourself that 'Call me in six months' is a good advance! It's nothing, Scott!" "So I'm sure you think you got an advance in that last call. Do you really believe that by doing yet another quote, it can be considered an advance? So what's the client doing in all of this anyway?" Great salespeople are not easily romanced into believing they received a good advance unless they have truly received a good advance. If they are in a call and their primary and secondary advances are not possible, they quickly think on the fly and develop an advance that is possible, and then they go for it. As hard as I believe great salespeople are on themselves, they are also the first to congratulate themselves on some quick thinking on the fly and the achieving of a great advance under the circumstances.

Let's spend a moment on the concept of advancing for advancing's sake. It's important to always question whether your advances are advancing the sales process in a defined direction that will lead to commitment. Sometimes advance after advance seems productive, yet in the end, those advances lead down yet another tangent. Always question yourself as to whether this next step is truly leading somewhere valuable for you as it specifically relates to getting an eventual commitment. Don't snow yourself! Your time is valuable, and if you feel like you are on a tangent, you probably are. Either probe the client to get back on track or toss in your hand!

INFORMATION OVERLOAD

A salesperson and a sales manager begin walking toward the car. The silence is finally broken when the salesperson says, "Wow, I can't believe how much information we received on that call! It was like someone finally opened up the flood gates at this account. All of my hard work finally paid off today. I suppose when it rains, it pours, and I loved getting drenched on that call today." The sales manager speaks up. "Well, *you* opened up those flood gates. Your information-gathering questions and your extender questions were flawless. You forfeited your ability to talk right from the start and listened instead. By the end, you were scoring points at will! It was one of the best sales calls I've ever been on with a salesperson, and it's rewarding to experience your growth in sales professionalism." The salesperson says, "I want to thank you for all of your mentoring and patience. I just love sales thanks in a large part to you!"

Could this be a dream? For many sales representatives, it is still a dream. It will be a dream come true if they have a never-ending passion for sales and a never-ending persistence to keep improving. The information-gathering phase to a sales call is every bit as important as the warm-up phase: good preparation, changing gears on the fly, great initial questions, and add-on questions, or extender questions, along with an uncanny ability to dig deep into problems, so deep the salesperson "drains the well." All of these concepts and others can produce great results. Certainly a willing customer with unresolved needs is an important ingredient in all of this success. How does a salesperson expose a willing customer? Very carefully—by providing a professional atmosphere and by being courteous, subservient, knowledgeable, truly concerned, prepared, and likable and any other trait described in a Boy Scout handbook. Once trust is earned, the flood gates can open up, and sometimes all at once you've got a flood on your hands. This type of flood is truly a good thing!

DON'T DRIVE OFF WITHOUT PAYING

At the time of this writing, gasoline prices are at an all-time high. It doesn't matter; you can't drive off without paying! The same is true at the end of a sales call. You can't drive off without "paying" attention to what happened in the sales event. How did it go? What could you have done better? What did you do poorly? Did everything go as planned, and why or why not? Were your perceptions correct? Did you get the advance you had planned, or did you get one at all? During the sales event, were you talking to a Waldo (decision maker), or did you get the name of the Waldo(s)? What's expected of you now that the sales event is over, and is it clear in both parties' minds? A quiet recap right after the sales event is vital to continued progress in sales. It doesn't matter whether you've sold for 10 years or one year; stop everything after the call and recap. Write down the names of the potential decision makers you uncovered before you forget them. Write down all the items you promised to accomplish so you remember to do them. Stay in "the zone" for a time after the call to make it a sincerely professional event. Write down the answers to the questions above in your account folder and check yourself on the ones below.

- Did I ask all the questions on my pre-call plan?
- Was I on time or five minutes late again?
- Was there enough time? Did I overstay my welcome?
- Could I have probed better on the phone before I made this appointment?
- How warm was the fire I built in the warm-up phase?
- Did I ask all the information-gathering questions I wanted to ask?
- Did I talk too much?
- Was the call an enjoyable event for both parties? Either party?
- Did anyone laugh? Did I create any rapport?
- Was I valuable in the client's eyes?
- Is this contact a prospect? Does he or she really have a desire to change something in the future that I can potentially solve with my products?
- Did I create a desire to continue? Or did I just fulfill an obligation to meet with me because I was able to make the appointment and that's it?

It's also important to confirm with the client *before* you leave what you've promised to follow up on. Get on the same page before you leave the sales event. This is the obvious part; follow up on every promise you make in the time frame you qualified as appropriate with the client. Don't fail here because you misunderstood what was promised or when your promise was expected. All sales books talk about trust and how important trust is in any profitable relationship. Well, isn't trust totally related to doing what you promised in the time frame you promised every time you promise? Yes. It's also about never over-promising. Truly believe you can provide every promise you make when you make it! If it turns out that for some reason you can't fulfill a promise you have made, not an over-promise you have made, then be honest with the customer and tell him or her as soon as you know you can't perform on a promise. Don't ever hide and hope it goes away—it won't! Apologize for any inconvenience it may have caused your client, and most important, be professional, honest, and forthright as soon as you know you can't perform on anything you promised.

THE POSTGAME INTERVIEW

We've all experienced postgame interviews after watching our favorite team contend in sporting event, or after a sporting event our child played in, or for that matter, any type of competition. It's usually a recap of what went well and what could have gone better shortly after the game has ended.

What percentage of the time do you conduct a postgame interview after you lose a sale? Oftentimes the salesperson's conversation goes like this: "No, it's all right; I understand. I thought you might choose XYZ for that job. Thank you very much for the opportunity and for considering our proposal. I really enjoyed meeting you, and hopefully, we can work together some day. Good luck and thanks again." Very few sales representatives go on to say:

- I'm curious as to what was so appealing about XYZ's proposal.
- What could I have done differently during the process to improve my position?

- I thought you preferred _____ about the other proposal. Were my **perceptions** correct?
- Could you offer me some advice about how I could have handled myself better from a professional standpoint?
- Who actually made the decision, and what swayed him or her to purchase XYZ?
- Are there any opportunities that do remain at this point?
- I hope it's OK to thank (deciding agent's name) for the chance to be considered on this opportunity after all the time and effort I put in.
- My perception was that XYZ offered _____ and that their _____ was _____. How far off is my **perception,** and is this what transpired?
- Our new ABC unit is very close to production. Could we set up a time to meet on it a month from now? I'm available on May 2 at 3:00 p.m.

The best salespeople have some of the most well-targeted **perceptions**. For them, the postgame interview is an opportunity to check out their **perceptions.** They love knowing what the score is at any given point in time and who's ahead in the race but, more important, who's ahead at the finish line specifically. This is their chance to check out their **perceptions** and whether they are off base and try to understand why.

The postgame interview is also a chance to obtain a green light to visit with the next level. "Would you mind if I called _____ and just thanked him/her?" Many times the processing agent will say yes then because he or she feels sorry you lost! Try it! It might work and get you that long-awaited appointment. It might be an opportunity to first thank but then also reiterate your desire to eventually win at their account and show how graciously you lose.

Using the postgame interview to try to reverse the decision is certainly a strategy, but most likely it will be the last strategy you will be able to use at that account. Go for broke if you don't care about ever doing business with the client again. Most likely your efforts will be futile and full of anxiety.

> *Set a percentage of time you will conduct a postgame interview—maybe 80% of the time—and stick to it. It's amazing what you will find out! Keep checking out your perceptions and see how correct they are as they relate to how and why the customer decided. The better you get at perceiving the true picture in your contests, the quicker you can react, reload, and change tactics and increase your winning percentages.*

KEEP PERCEIVING AND PRACTICING

The art of a great face-to-face sales event is exactly that: an art form. When it happens, it's like a long gymnastic routine at the Olympics when a contestant nails everything, including the dismount, and gets all 10s. Hopefully these past chapters have helped and/or reinforced your current strategies. Excellence in sales is a never-ending process no matter how many years you have sold. All of us can always get better in sales in some way or another. The day any of us feels as though we know everything is the day our growth in the sales profession—and our income—is stunted. Perceive what cards have been played, verify your perceptions with the client, and never stop counting cards during any of the games you decide to play. Again, it's just as important to throw in your hand if you feel you are overmatched. Then you can devote your valuable time elsewhere. Learn from the hands you were going to throw in but didn't and instead won. Those hands are truly the ones deserving of a closer look. Increasing your winning percentages on those hands will put money in your savings account, not just your checking account!

NON-FACE-TO-FACE SELLING STRATEGIES II

STRATEGICALLY SPEAKING IN SALES

So you've made yet another great sales call. Wow, all these great sales calls in a row! When will your string be broken? It's the day after your last great sales call; in fact, there's not a chance your string will be broken today because you don't have a sales call scheduled for today! And what does that mean? That the celebration can last for yet another day! Something to be happy about? I don't think so!

These next few chapters relate to how strategically you and I use our time when we're not making sales calls—you know, all that other time, the time in between making face-to-face sales calls. Actually, it works out to be 70% of our time for the average salesperson. Now, that's a lot of time! We could accomplish a great deal with all that time, couldn't we?

THE PROCESSING AGENT

"All the orders at XYZ company come (get processed) through me!" "I purchase (process) all the _____ for this company!" "You'll have to stop in the purchasing department (to be processed) before you go anywhere!" "I'm responsible for (I process) all the RFPs." How many times have you heard these statements in your sales career? Most likely, many times. **Salespeople are not looking for people who "process" decisions that others have already made! Great salespeople are constantly in a search of the people who decide which orders will actually get processed by the processing agent!**

So many salespeople are perfectly content calling and, worse yet, relying on the people who process decisions for their livelihood in sales. They are always hoping these people will bring home the order for them. They start at accounts in the processing department and are forever trying to move past the obstacle they created in the first place. It's important to find out in advance *who* decides on what *is* processed at a particular targeted account (i.e., the decision maker, Waldo, the manager behind the real wood desk, the tiebreaker at the account, etc.) and start there! Many books call these people a variety of different names, but what's important is that you treat finding the people who make the decisions at the account like an obsession! Begin with the people who will actually use the products that get processed or the people who's job is on the line for the results of the products that get processed. These are the people who salespeople need to exploit at their accounts. Certainly there are times when processing agents are also deciding agents, but believe it or not, this happens very infrequently. Start at the deciding agent level; seek them out. If you're pushed down to the processing agent level, fine, but hopefully not before you get a word in edgewise with the deciding agent or at least a chance to meet him or her before going downstairs to the processing department!

How do you pick out deciding agents? Well, you have to be quick because they are usually in a hurry. You'll have to be prepared because they will have time for only a few facts. You'll have to create a lasting impression fast by being professional, articulate, and valuable. They will be well insulated, with many "gatekeepers" in your way. Whenever you're researching the account or are at the account, you turn your radar up high and make sure you either carefully probe for the name or pick the name out of a flurry of 100 other words that are said at any given time. Network with others inside the account or outside the account, but seek out the name(s) of the decision makers at your accounts. We will talk later in this book about how to get to these people, but for now, let's agree to turn up the heat as to knowing the deciding agents at every one of your accounts and writing the names down in your account folder.

- Bill, could you help me understand who gets involved in the decisions at XYZ?

- Bill, everyone has told me that I have to talk to Sherri if I want to make things happen. What's Sherri's role, and why is she so influential? Could you help me meet her someday?
- Bill, my company wants me to meet the president at XYZ. I know the president doesn't decide on my types of items specifically, or does he/she? It's my impression that someone other than the president and, of course, you, is influential.
- Bill, I appreciate you taking my proposal to _____. Could I come with you when you do? Could we propose together? Well, could you at least tell me who you need to sell on my proposal and what makes him/her tick?
- Bill, I'm sure you're fully aware of the pressure my management places on me to meet so-and-so. Could we brainstorm on how to make this happen together?

The reason I came up with some of these questions is because the processing agent is so many times also the middleman. As we all know, it's tough to bypass the middleman. The middleman works very hard not to be perceived as the middleman. Many salespeople have first-hand experience with being the middleman themselves, and they fight hard to hold on to their position and justify it. The processing agent is in the same position, and great salespeople understand these similarities. They develop an artful way of embracing the situation and getting to the deciding agents without burning any bridges. Salespeople realize it can take time, persistence, and a constant determination to qualify themselves to be in a position to move up. They also know it is far easier to start at the deciding agent level in the first place, professionally qualify themselves, and be so valuable that they stay with the deciding agent(s) throughout their tenure at the account.

THE INNER CIRCLE

Most salespeople can remember a great sale they have made in their past. The big one, the tough one, the one that didn't get away! *They* were the one the client called for information during what seemed like every day at the time. *They* were the salesperson who the client showed the most trust and confidence. *They* were the benchmark at the account. *They* laughed and joked with the client about what the competition was trying to do to catch up. *They* told their sales manager it was in the bag, a slam dunk, game, set, match, and they were right! *These* salespeople were in the "inner circle"!

The inner circle is a great place, a place every salesperson strives to enjoy on every opportunity. It's a place where you are selling but it's gotten so easy it doesn't feel like you're selling anymore. Salespeople want so badly to believe they are in the inner circle that they tend to talk themselves and their managers into believing that they have arrived even though they haven't. Bottom line: only the salespeople themselves know how close they really are to that coveted inner circle experience on any given account or what it will take to break in. It's important that salespeople are honest with themselves and their managers. If it doesn't feel like the time you won the "big one," then it isn't. Don't sugarcoat it; it is what it is. You have to decide first whether to spend time breaking in, what your chances of breaking in are, and how best to break in. Sometimes no matter how hard you try, the stars and the moon will never align at the account or opportunity. It will always seem like you're riding in the backseat! If you've earned the right to ask some of the questions below, then ask them and stop wondering.

Salesperson:	I've never felt as though I'm in the "inner circle" at this account. I've tried for a long time, but I just feel as though I have never broken in. Is there a reason for this feeling in your opinion? Please, be honest with me!
Client:	Well, we've purchased from Bill for years, and Bill is Jean's cousin, so, I guess—
	Or
	We honestly just like buying from XYZ. It's fast, easy, and hassle free.
	Or
	I think you've been trying to break into the wrong circle!
	Or
	I'll tell you: if you want to break in, Judy holds the key!
	Or
	You'll never break in! We just don't hit if off, and I will never forget the chance I gave you several years ago.

Take all of these answers like a professional and decide what to do next, understanding your time is very valuable.

OK. Let's say you've arrived, and you are officially in the inner circle with *both* feet. It's great; orders are flowing in almost effortlessly, and you rely on this cash cow to make your goals every month or maybe every year. You are officially what some call fat and happy! Not to burst your bubble so quickly, but fat and happy is a dangerous, vulnerable position. *Remember playing "king of the hill" when you were a kid? Well, usually the "king" got knocked off. It may have taken some time, but eventually the "king" gets knocked off the hill.* It's no different in sales. Always, always, always keep selling even your best accounts and never, never, never rest on your laurels unless these laurels are the constant value you keep bringing to the account every day! Service the account like it was your first day you broke into the inner circle. Remember that all things end—yes, all things end. Plan for the end. Before the end, try to break into another inner circle at another account while you brainstorm with your current inner circle account on how to create a new horizon of values. Hold off your competitor as long as you can because when you get knocked off the hill, only you know how tough it will be to get on top again! The best of luck to you, oh, king of many hills!

THE CART BEFORE THE HORSE

When people talk about placing the cart before the horse, they usually laugh about it, and then they decide to calm down, reload, and retrace their steps and begin to move forward again. Let's take a moment to picture the cart before the horse. Let's picture the horse pushing the cart. It would be almost as difficult as a salesperson "pushing" clients into action all day long, every day of every week for a whole year. Imagine how difficult it would be for the horse and that salesperson. It is far easier to take the horse around to the front of the cart, hitch it up to the cart, and let the horse pull the cart—almost as easy as it would be for a salesperson to be sitting at his or her desk with a nice cup of coffee on a beautiful day only to have the phone ring with a large prospect on the phone who is asking for an appointment soon because of the proposal that was just dropped off. Oh, the differences between pushing and pulling in sales, almost as different as night and day.

The amount of time spent pushing in a sales career varies by hour, by day, by week, by year. But pushing, if it isn't the present task at hand, is the dreadful task lurking around the corner of each and every day in sales. Pushing is tough. It's disliked by even the best sales representatives. But without pushing, even the best sales representatives fail. It's simply the worst part about sales. It's why people fail in sales. It's why some people hate sales. It's why some people get out of sales. The constant pressure to push others and generate new opportunities on an ongoing basis is not for everyone. This type of pushing is not so much pushing people to buy but pushing people to see you, talk to you, let you propose, give you a chance to perform, trust you over the incumbent vendor—pushing people to start with you and desire to continue with you.

I offer a couple of secrets to help embrace this dreadful part of sales:

- **First, realize and embrace that pushing will be an everyday part of your job in sales.** If your title has everything to do with sales or it's a part of what you are required to do, realize that pushing is here to stay. Decide today, if you haven't by now, to embrace pushing. Otherwise, you should get out of sales because if you don't embrace pushing, you'll never be good at sales, and it might be best to work in another profession.
- **The amount of pushing you have to do on an ongoing basis should change in percentage of time.** Some days, weeks, and, yes, even years, this pushing percentage of your time is very high. Keep it high, be persistent, take breaks, and escape, but come right back to it. Don't procrastinate; it won't go away. It's here to stay! If you **do** get a little pull from some clients, don't let it fool you into believing that you'll never have to push again. All your pushing will have an effect, just not a long-lasting effect. If after a year of pushing your percentage remains high, above 50% of your allowable time, something might be wrong. Either all this pushing isn't working or you're pushing wrong. Certainly don't wait an entire year to ask for help, but it's important to get some expert advice along the way to see

whether you are on the right track or ask about the percentages of time spent pushing during the interview process.

- **Spend time developing a strategic plan or plans for pushing.** Work your plans and be persistent. To be good at pushing, it is going to take a strategic plan. Develop a target list or lists. Systematically work your plans (Plan A, Plan B, Plan C, Plan D, etc.) and stay focused on the parameters associated with these plans you have decided upon. It's critical to develop a system of tracking that works and that you believe in. It doesn't matter whether it's an automated or a manual system; embrace it and believe that it will work. Make sure it has a great follow-up system so anytime you say you will follow up, you do in fact follow up as promised.
- **Cherish any chance you do get to be pulled by your prospects.** Enjoy the chance to react to being pulled. Perform impeccably in this opportunity and be professional. Celebrate the fact that all this pushing has resulted in a pull or two! Sometimes pulling takes over for a while, and it's easy to forget about pushing all together, especially because pushing is such a "loved" activity! The best salespeople are always mixing pushing with pulling, and they realize that they must always be loading their sales funnel or the funnel eventually runs dry and so does their checking account.
- **Develop a "proactive list" of potential prospects on a separate pad of paper.** This list is a group of people who relate to a particular plan you developed, and the list comprises of the name of the account, the name of contact, the phone numbers associated with that prospect, and any notes. The best salespeople pull this list out on the fly and call on it while they are on the move. **Or they designate a time in the office each week to be "proactive time," and all they do is call on their proactive list *and nothing else—nothing*!**

- **Set realistic goals for yourself so in the end you can kick yourself in the butt when you don't live up to your expectations.** The worst thing you can do is decide on a plan of attack, set unrealistic goals, and say to yourself when you are done, "I didn't think I could do it, and guess what? I didn't! Oh, well." Realistic goals will change all this, and at the end, you'll say something different: "That's not acceptable. I purposefully reduced my expectations to a reasonable level, and I still failed. Enough is enough! I will not fail again." Then you'll kick yourself in the butt!
- **Your plan of attack has to have a time frame attached to it.** I like to use a quarterly time frame. Each quarter I like to accomplish a particular plan of attack. Three months' time is usually enough time to complete a plan and be able to kick myself in the butt if I don't complete it.

Pushing, prospecting, promoting, being proactive—they all have to consume your thinking day in and day out. The best salespeople prospect the most! They make time to prospect. They save time to prospect. They create time to prospect. They fall asleep thinking about prospecting and wake up thinking about prospecting!

GONE FISHING

"Great! The engine started," said Carl as he loaded his gear into the boat. "Yeah, new plugs, new gas, and a charged-up battery do the trick every time," responded Brad. The two loaded up for a beautiful day of fishing. After venturing through the channel, the large lake was finally ahead of them. "Let's go right to the middle and fish!" said Carl. Brad thought for a while and said, "Maybe they are biting over near that nudist camp again?" "Yeah, now that's a good idea. Let's troll over there for a while," said Carl. The two motored over toward the camp and trolled along the shore. "Quite the view!" said Carl. Brad said, "Carl, eyes on the water, buddy." "I've seen enough. Let's fish over near all those other boats," said Brad. They pulled in their lines, started the motor, and headed toward the other boats. People all around them were catching fish, but Brad and Carl were just thirsty and casting. "Wonder what lure they are using to catch all those fish?" said Carl. Brad reached for his tackle box and pulled out the biggest, brightest lure in the box. "This should do the trick!" said Brad. Carl stuck with a smaller lure, the same one he had used for years regardless of which lake they fished on or what time of the year they fished or what type of fish were biting. "Finally!" said Carl as he got a strike and started to reel in as fast as he could. It wasn't long before the fish was gone and only weeds were left on Carl's hook. Brad said to Carl after he lost the fish, "Carl, you have to set the hook after you get a strike. As soon as you feel the strike, tug hard and set the hook deep in the fish." "Set the hook? At least I got a strike! Fish on your own side of the boat, Bradman," said Carl. Now it was time for Brad to get a strike. He quickly tugged on his rod to set the hook and slowly reeled the fish closer. Sometimes Brad let the line run out; other times he reeled in slowly. But slowly but surely, the fish got closer and closer to the boat. "Get the net, Carl," said Brad. Carl got the net and eased it in the water as Brad maneuvered the fish in close. Then before Brad knew it, the fish shot under the boat, and a second later, it was gone! "We were so close! Did you see how big that one was?" Brad said in disappointment. Carl just smiled and said, "Guess you didn't set the hook! I'm thirsty!"

Sales can be very much like fishing in many respects. Where do you go to catch the biggest fish in sales? It's important to always be very strategic about where you sell and why you sell there. Make sure you always fish where the fish are biting and people are catching fish! Some accounts will never buy, and they will waste hours of your valuable time. Great salespeople ask some great questions like:

- How much would you say you spend on X each year?
- Now that you've purchased an XYZ system, when will you be in the market again for an ABC?
- I've been calling on you for almost six months now, and quite honestly I don't think I'm any closer to getting an order than I was on day one. What do you think my chances are of making a sale here?

- You've purchased XYZ for years. What are the chances of purchasing some of my solutions over time, and why would you feel they would be more valuable to you over time?

The best salespeople are always qualifying their time and efforts to make sure they are moving in the right direction, the direction of making a sale and getting the fish in the boat! They constantly check out their chances of winning as well as how soon they might win.

A great fisherman is also very persistent. Cast after cast after cast, from sunup to sundown some days. Salespeople generally are not persistent enough to reap real benefits. They call a couple times, and then it's off to something else. The best salespeople develop strategies that take them back to key strategically chosen customers time after time until they win or *truly* decide it's a dead end. Generally, salespeople don't truly decide a customer is a "dud." They just give up before they ever get to that point. They will go to the account two times but not six times, especially if there is no immediate, clear indication of an interest to purchase anything specific. They have trouble coming up with justification to see the customer those last four times and usually move on because of it. The best salespeople see potential on those first two calls because of artful probing and are kicking themselves in the butt for not making faster progress on tapping that potential. They continue to develop new strategies to legitimize the third, fourth, and fifth calls and strike a deal on the sixth call. Each call builds on the previous call, and eventual penetration of the account is the usual outcome. These great salespeople are very perceptive at analyzing the situation during and after each call to decide whether they are wasting their precious time. And their time is precious! In fact, they know exactly how much they must sell to justify each hour of precious face-to-face sales time. These great salespeople are always concerned about the return on their invested time—especially after six calls of no sales at a particular account, they are very concerned about their use of time, and they analyze their every step. But they also understand that it is really tough to knock the incumbent out of office, and they have to work twice as hard to do so and they JUST DO IT!

What lure do you use? Most tackle boxes are full of all sorts of lures. The question is, Which one do you use? Depends on the lake, depends on the time of the season, depends on which fish are biting that particular day. It's important not to choose the lure (solution) before you learn everything you can about your client. So often salespeople will present solutions the client isn't interested in purchasing.

- If you were me, where would you start at your account?
- Are there any areas where you still haven't found just the right solution?
- It seems to me that it would be best to propose our XYZ solution. What do you think?
- I honestly don't think we have a match here. Do you agree? Maybe I should call you after the New Year after you've had a chance to _____.

If you don't find the right lure (solution) in the tackle box, then face it and wait for another day. Don't waste your time by fishing with the wrong lure! You'll waste your valuable time and the client's. Probe hard on what lure makes the most sense and cast with that lure. Always ask what price is acceptable as well. Obviously it's important to sell value, not price, but value and price are tied together just like a fishing lure and the fishing line itself. If the fish are biting on worms that day, then fish with worms; even the most expensive lure won't work if the fish want worms.

"Setting the hook" is essential in sales, as it is in fishing. If there is true interest on behalf of the customer, then set the hook by presenting a proposal, put a stake in the ground, and talk about specific dollars, specific time frames, and specific features and benefits as a solution to the desire you've created. Get the customer looking at specifics and begin reeling the fish toward the boat! Just because you have set the hook and have begun reeling the fish toward the boat doesn't mean you will be able to get the fish in the boat! All that counts is the number of fish you actually get in the boat! So many salespeople talk about how big the fish was while it was in the water or how close to the boat it was or how many strikes they had that day—or else they are constantly blaming their lack of success on all sorts of things other than themselves. These salespeople are also the ones who always paint a bright picture of the future, but when the future becomes the present, it's never as bright as it was going to be months or years earlier. Develop a will to win and get the fish in the boat!

Fish in strategic spots where other people are catching fish or better yet where you are the only one catching fish! Strategically choose lures (solutions) that make sense and that catch fish on that particular day (client). If you feel a nibble on the line, set the hook and propose real specifics. After the hook is set, slowly reel in the customer with constant attention and concern until you get the fish in the boat. Only when the fish is in the boat is it time to celebrate! Keep your excitement subdued until the fish is in the boat! Then and only then is it time to reach for the fish scale and weigh your prize catch and reach for a "cold one"!

May your boat always be full of fish!

PINBALL WIZARD

Most likely your knowledge of and amusement from pinball machines depends on your age. My 19-year-old probably has never played a pinball machine, and by 19 years of age, I played several of my favorite machines every weekend. In those days, the trick was to tilt the machine ever so slightly to coerce the ball out of one area and into another. Wasn't it fun to watch the pinball wizards! I was never a wizard. A true wizard had his or her name or initials on the top 10 list the machine would post at the end of great games. The true wizard of all wizards would be listed several times on that list. Sometimes I was at the machine when the wizard was playing. That was a sight to see. The ball would bounce around like it was made of rubber. The saves before the ball would be lost were unbelievable. The wizard's ability to get the ball over toward the bonus area was uncanny. More than anything, the wizard's ability to bounce the ball numerous times off the 100-point bumpers was where his or her points were scored. I could create the same flurry of action, but at the end of the game, I would look up only to be disappointed with my results and how far I was from my burning desire to put my initials into the machine. Now the wizard, however, he or she would create the same flurry, but at the end of the game, his or her score was yet another opportunity to place initials in the top 10.

This scenario reminds me of salespeople to a certain extent. Some salespeople seem like they always create a flurry of action, but in the end, when they look up, their score isn't anywhere near that of the wizards on their sales team. Sometimes it's because these salespeople are bouncing off the five- and 10-point clients all game long, and these clients demand the same flurry of action as 100-point clients, but in the end the points simply don't add up to a top 10 game. Sometimes these salespeople are afraid of the 100-point clients for whatever reason, and they are just more comfortable with five- and 10-point customers. Maybe it's because these salespeople have tried the 100-point clients and the experience was unpleasant and in the end a waste of time and so they never went back again. Sometimes these salespeople quite honestly don't know which clients are 100-point customers and truly see a bumper to be a bumper. Or these salespeople have a favorite 100-point client but for a variety of reasons can't seem to get the ball over to that area to generate points or can't find any more 100-point clients.

Salespeople must first develop a template of questions they continually ask of clients in hot pursuit of deciding how many points they can score by hitting on that client's bumper.

- What would you say your budget is for those types of widgets each year?
- In an ideal world, how many of those would you purchase in any given year?

- If I were to break in and become the alternative vendor, about how much business would that be worth every year in general terms, and what percentage of the pie does that represent?
- Does that mean your situation has changed for this year and you won't purchase till next year?
- With all of that in mind, do you think you will have any money to purchase any of my solutions this year?

Salespeople must aggressively research what a 100-point customer looks like. They must interview wizards on their sales staff, look at leads, research their territory, consider new trends that might be appearing—**anything required to list these large accounts with confidence in the first place**.

Salespeople must then have the confidence to attack that list. Begin by setting Mr. Pro Crastination aside and attack! Jump in the water! Get out of the stands and on the field! Become a heat-seeking missile and find the target! Clients don't bite; dogs do. Get an appointment with these large 100-point clients and don't stop until you are successful. Everyone will eventually see anyone once. When it's your time, be prepared, ask good questions, set a value on that bumper, decide whether it's valuable, and then get your ball over to that account!

If you are new at sales, it's OK, at least initially, to set 100-point customers over to the side until you're ready or confident—just as long as you become ready and confident in the foreseeable future! Become ready and confident as quickly as you can and maybe start with the easiest 100-point customer first, but don't become fat and happy and stop there! Remember, you will never be happy, your sales manager will never be happy, and your family will never be happy with you bouncing off five- and 10-point customers.

Don't shoot rabbits with your elephant gun! Sometimes salespeople represent companies that lead or dominate their markets nationwide. Some salespeople across the nation are dropping elephants left and right with *their* elephant guns. If you have the same gun and you're not dropping elephants in time, something is wrong. It's not that your market is different from theirs and it's not that this is different or that is different; usually *you* are the one who is really different. Don't be afraid to face the facts and decide that it's not the gun. You just can't shoot elephants, at least not yet! Decide to work hard and smart on several large 100-point accounts and **drop a damn elephant with the elephant gun you've been given!**

EXPOSE THE SCOREBOARD

Certainly some of us have either watched our own kids play soccer or we will some day. Most, if not all, soccer fields for young kids don't have actual scoreboards. Maybe it's an issue of cost, or maybe it relates to the actual number of goals scored in each game. One parent turns to another on a sunny day in spring and says, "Is the score 1–1 or is it 2–1?" It's simply tough in higher-scoring sports to survive without a scoreboard of some sort. Sometimes the scoreboard lets you go home early and beat the traffic. Sometimes the scoreboard makes you feel like you got your money's worth at the contest. Sometimes the scoreboard allows you to catch up if you've drifted off for a while. Wouldn't it be great if the score was posted in sales? At any given point in time, you could look up and tell how far in front or behind you were in that particular opportunity. With a scoreboard, it would also be clear how many competitors were in your contests at any given point in time. Scoreboards are simply very valuable and pack a great deal of information vital to being able to track the outcome of the game. If the scores in your current opportunities were posted somewhere, would they change your strategies in those opportunities?

It's always surprising how many sales representatives are afraid to ask for the score at any given time in the sales process. No matter whether the sales process has just begun or is nearing the end, there is always a score! Let's say you're trying to replace an incumbent supplier or take share away from him or her. There is a score; that supplier is ahead, and you're behind. Even if the opportunity is at the beginning phases and there is no real incumbent, oftentimes the customer has some initial preferences, experiences, or history that has an early effect on the score. Certainly the score could be 0–0 at the beginning, but never assume that just because it is the beginning of the game.

Take the cover off the scoreboard every chance you get during the sales process.

- I get the feeling I'm in second place right now.
- It just seems to me that I'm in the race but am not going to win.
- I feel like I'm in first place right now, but I'm really not sure.
- Maybe I'm off in left field, but I believe (Competitor 1) will win this, (Competitor 2) will win that, and I will win this.
- If this game was over today, who would win?
- By the way, I think you said a while back that you would decide by November 1. Is that still the finish line?

Obviously, these are just a few of the questions that could be asked to analyze what the scoreboard currently looks like in the eyes of the customer. The point here is to ask these questions and obtain the clearest possible picture of the scoreboard. Probably just as important as asking the question is the answer you receive when the question is asked.

- I'm not really sure how "they" are thinking right now.
- I think you're in first, but it's really up to the committee.
- If it were up to me, _____.
- The last time "they" met, _____.

By asking score-like questions, you should be able to realize whether you are calling on a deciding agent or processing agent. Obviously, deciding agents know the score because they are the ones deciding who will win!

When you ask score questions, you might receive answers like this:

Client:	"Quite honestly, you're right. Your proposal isn't high on our list. We are leaning toward two others, and I really didn't know how to tell you."
Salesperson:	"No problem. I understand. What could I do to catch up at this point?"
Client:	"I'm sorry but probably not anything."
Salesperson:	"Tell me, if you would, how did my competitors get so far out in front?" "What should I have done differently?" "Who actually will decide?"

Questions about the score can be fascinating and can create the intrigue great salespeople thrive on every day. A true sales professional perceives the score in every contest and, more important, perceives the correct score. When a win or loss occurs, it's usually of no surprise to the best sales professionals. These same professionals have accomplished everything they set out to do before the decision is actually made, so there are no regrets at the end when the clock reads 00:00.

WIN, PLACE, OR SHOW

The horses and jockeys are entering the track now. The crowd is abuzz with excitement. It should be a great race today. Sixteen horses are entered. Anything can happen after last week's outcome when the long shot beat the favorite. Today those two will be at it again. Soon all the horses are in the gate, and quickly after the gates are filled, the bell rings. The horses leap forward, and the pack heads for turn 1. After turns 1 and 2, the pack of horses is pretty much still together. It's only after turn 3 that the three lead horses begin to pull away. As expected, the favorite, the long shot, and another horse begin to make it a three-horse race. They have rounded turn 4, and the home stretch is ahead. Any horse could win, but the long shot is still ahead. The favorite has taken his familiar position on the outside, and it should be a great finish. The long shot's one-horse-length lead is diminishing, and the finish line is getting closer and closer. The photo finish is a reality, and it looks like the favorite edged out the long shot by a nose. Yes, the long shot came in second after another very strong race. The favorite has held on by a nose. The people begin to move toward the pay-out windows to collect their proceeds. Certainly the favorite won the race—but not at the pay-out window. The people who placed bets on the "place and show" horses are winning at the pay-out windows for sure. So, who is the real winner?

Certainly, in many selling situations, a salesperson either wins or loses. Selling automobiles is probably the most familiar time for all of us when a salesperson would either get the sale or not. In many other selling situations, there might be several winners. Great salespeople are fully aware of the "win, place, or show" scenario in selling. They position themselves for the win, of course; however, they are also positioning themselves for a place or show finish at the same time. The best salespeople are always positioning themselves to be in the money by being in first, second, or third in all of the contests they decide to enter and spend their valuable time racing in. They are seldom in fourth place and finish out of the money. They are very savvy as to their chances of ending the race in the money and are always deciding whether to strategically continue or how much time to spend based on the return on their time invested. It's no different from a having a bad hand in cards when a player decides to throw in. Certainly the downside to throwing in or stepping away from a sales event becomes a "no sale." "No sales" don't add up to very much at the end of the year. Great salespeople are entered in enough races that a "no sale" here and there doesn't hinder them from blowing away their goal at the end of any given year.

Sometimes it's best to enter a race with a particular goal in mind, for example, not to win but to finish in the place or show position. These salespeople then let everyone know up front that their interests lie in that particular area, and they pour their efforts into that area. This decision might relate to an interest in higher profit margins, a lack of time available at the present time to try for more, or a decision not to take on the incumbent head on in *this* particular race.

Some salespeople are not as discerning as they should be about the races they decide to enter. Before they decide to invest their valuable time, they need to truly objectively analyze their chances of winning or coming in at the end of the race in the money. Oftentimes they get into somewhat of a frenzy and believe their chances of being in the money are greater than they really are in a particular race. They invest a great deal of time early and become committed, and when it may be time to pull out, they can't because of the time they have already invested. It's very important that throughout the entire sales process, beginning to end, there is a constant effort to probe for information as it relates to win, place, or show—or in other terms, being in the money. Obtaining tangible return for time invested is all important. So many times salespeople after a loss try to justify their efforts and time wasted by saying, "Well, at least I _____" or "I thought I would be able to _____" or "No one could have controlled those series of events." Whatever the excuse might be, it's still valuable time spent without reward, and in sales that *is* the kiss of death or *will eventually be* the kiss of death.

> *Choose your races wisely not only when you decide to enter at the beginning but also all the way through your races. How valuable is your time? Do you know? How much does it cost you to be in front of a customer for an hour face to face? What was that cost last year? What is it this year?*

IT'S TIED, AND IT'S OVERTIME

It doesn't matter whether you're a sports fanatic or you've seen a few games with personal interest over the years; the overtime period is exciting. Sometimes regulation ends after both teams have battled evenly through the entire contest in a true seesaw battle. Sometimes one team frantically makes a push at the end, and low and behold the score is tied after regulation. Some teams blow commanding leads. They begin resting on their laurels during the game, and confidence abounds, and when momentum shifts, they can't restart their engine, and before they know it, the score is tied! Mr. Mo Mentum is handing out high fives on *the competition's* sideline!

What's fascinating about sales is that no one actually posts a scoreboard. A salesperson can't look up at the scoreboard and see the list of competitors and verify that he or she is tied for first place. All salespeople can do is surmise the score on the basis of their probing, relationships, sales calls, proposals, perceptions, etc. Let's just say we knew the score; it really was tied, and the end of the game was next week at noon on Tuesday, and you've just arrived at your office on Friday morning.

It's amazing how many salespeople are "out of breath" at the end of regulation. They seem like the team that frantically performed at the end of the game to achieve a tie, and they are relieved and happy it's tied. Out of breath, they call their sales manager and say, "Well, it's down to two of us, and they will decide on Tuesday at noon." Usually there is a short period of silence, quick celebration over making the final cut, and then, the salesperson often says, "Well, I guess we will wait till Tuesday to find out whether we win." The sales manager says, "Enjoy your weekend if you can! Nice job! Hopefully, we will be celebrating on Tuesday."

The best salespeople say, "Great! Tuesday at noon. At least that gives me some more time. I have one competitor to beat, and here's what I'm going to do next. If I could get a meeting with _____ on Monday, maybe I could actually win this game!" It's called "will to win." The best salespeople roll into action. They cherish having some extra time on the clock to try a couple more strategies. It's almost like they have actually saved some energy for the end. They want Mr. Mo Mentum on their sideline! They are active and innovative right up to the end of overtime, Tuesday at noon. The best salespeople resemble a long-distance runner with a kick at the end of a 26-mile race. They call their sales manager at noon on Tuesday and say, "Well, I had a great meeting with _____, changed my proposal to take one last shot at my competitor right where he/she is weakest, and wrote a note to _____ with my personal commitment to serve the company and expressed my appreciation for the opportunity to perform." Then this salesperson goes to his or her favorite quiet spot and says to himself or herself quietly, "I have truly done everything I can. Now, I'm at peace with myself. I can wait for the decision. May the best package win!"

Is this salesperson "waiting to lose"? No way! He or she may in fact lose but surely didn't wait to lose! Always, always do everything you can before the end of the game. Never accept "I've done everything I can do." *If there is time left on the clock, there is always something to do. Always do it, and don't just talk about doing it!*

WAITING TO LOSE

Your sales manager calls. It's late in the day, and he wants to go over your project list. You're on the phone with him, and he can't see you roll your eyes, so you roll away. You again make your quick but futile efforts to change the subject. It's no good; it's that dreadful time again. You start praying you can find your list and pass yet another test. The discussions over your project list start, and the two of you banter away. Advances, "I'll checks," and some "We won" are mixed into the discussion, and then, the "such-and-such" project comes up again. You hate to talk about this one. It's big and high profile, and you're upset it's even on the radar screen! You vowed to bury it somewhere, just not on this list! Any list—but not this one! Worse yet, you haven't done anything on it since the last time the two of you talked about it. Here it comes: "So what's happening on the 'such-and-such' project?" your manager asks. You start to talk—well, it's really more like babble! You begin to promise all sorts of next steps, and worse yet, you really don't know what your manager thinks you know, and you're afraid to be honest. Please let it be time for the next project—please! **Welcome to "waiting to lose."**

This is the project you are *hoping* will turn your way. You try to convince yourself that it's not time yet, but you know you've been convincing yourself of that for so long it probably *is* time! You *think* there is no chance of winning, but you don't have the guts to tell your manager or find out for yourself whether you are right or wrong. The client and you don't get along, but you don't want to tell anyone that you can't get along with someone, especially someone at such a large opportunity. You dropped items off long ago, and you are still hanging on to that feeble, lackluster effort, but in the eyes of everyone else who is viewing the radar screen, it's legitimate. You're afraid, *aggressively* procrastinating, and **WAITING TO LOSE**!

Get off your butt and do something! Now! Not tomorrow, today! Call the client now! Not next week! Now! Set up an appointment now or leave a voice mail message now! Commit to follow up on that voice mail later today! Place this opportunity at the top of your list now! If this project is a lemon, find out now, find out for sure, and find out where you are in the race now! If you are in eighth place in an eight-horse race, fine, but find out! While you are at it, find out where the finish line is and whether there is still time to finish in the money. Don't let the anxiety over this project drain another ounce of energy out of you. Do something significant now! Remember: you're a sales professional! Perform like one!

Aggressively get to a point in these types of projects where you honestly feel you have done everything you can do to win the project for the company you represent! If it's a loss, then so be it! Be proud of the fact that you got off your butt, finally, and found out what was going on and that you are not waiting to lose any longer. Never again wait to lose on any project! Never!

HOW WELL DO YOU WAIT?

"Let's *wait* until next Tuesday." "There's nothing else to do now but *wait*." "We should *wait* until the committee meets." "They will decide on Friday; let's *wait* and see." "The best option is to just *wait* till _____." Wait, wait, and wait! All this waiting gets on great salespeople's nerves. The best salespeople can't stand waiting and hate when waiting is an option, especially their only option. In fact, for them, they equate waiting to failure. It almost seems that "wait" isn't in their vocabulary. "There must be something I can do other than just wait!" "Heck, there is no way I'm waiting till Tuesday. I'm going to do this and this before Tuesday, and at least by Tuesday I will have done everything I could have done." "If *you* feel comfortable waiting till Tuesday, fine, but I don't; I'm going to try one more thing before the finish line appears!" "I think the *worst* thing we can do is wait right now! Do you actually think our competition is waiting right now? No way! It doesn't matter what everyone else is doing; here's what we're going to do." It's almost like the word "wait" means "no way" to these salespeople and the sheer thought of waiting spurs them into action instead of non-action. They just don't wait well!

Before you settle in on waiting as your next step, decide to check out every other possible action that could be taken other than waiting and decide and take action on one of them. Horses don't wait in a photo finish horse race; they are running like mad at the end, and their jockey is using his stick with great abandon. Competitors, at least good ones, don't settle for waiting at the end, either. They jockey for position, and they go down swinging.

If you ever decide to wait, it should be only after you have exhausted all other options. Remember: never is your best option to wait, and always feel uncomfortable when you have decided that waiting is better than taking any other strategic step. Waiting is for wimps! Cast the thought of waiting aside forever!

SELF-TALK RADIO

As a sales manager over the years, I have probably sat "shotgun" in a salesperson's car more than 100 times in the recent past. I'd say 80% of the time the radio was on when I got in the car. Not a bad thing, just an annoying thing for me. Most obvious is the fact that when the radio is on, it's simply hard to talk. So most of the time one of us turned it down very quickly and began to strategize together about the day and throughout the day. It's funny—we never turned the radio on again the rest of the day. Why? Well, you can't concentrate on your job or strategize about the next call with the radio on! As anal as this might sound, the level of your professionalism, as it relates to your sales job, begins right here. The minute you get in your car in the morning, begin concentrating on the day. What will you accomplish? What will you solve and cross off your list today? You will by the end of the day make an appointment with so-and-so because you *will* call him or her eight times today. Today as you drive, you *will* develop a plan to solve some of your major problems. Today as you drive, you *will* decide how to handle that difficult personal issue. Today, you *will* decide what you will do as it relates to the situation with that fellow employee you had a run in with last week. Today as you drive, you *will* get in a zone and stay in that zone and mentally strategize on your success in sales. I believe improved success in sales could relate to this simple change in your daily routine. The best salespeople simply strategize the most. They utilize their drive and flight time to accomplish a great deal more every day, both mentally and physically.

Now that I've asked you to give up your favorite daytime radio shows, wait till you hear what's next. Is it time to skip to the next chapter? No way! Hear me out on this very important subject as it relates to your success. Now that it is quiet in your car right now as you drive along, begin by enjoying the quiet. Cherish it. Maybe it is a beautiful day—take it in. Think how lucky you are to be out today instead of stuck in an office somewhere all day. **If this chapter isn't weird enough, it's now time for self-talk.** We all talk to ourselves. It's just that some people fill their thoughts with negative thoughts and others fill their thoughts with positive thoughts! It's important to use this newfound quiet time to talk to yourself with positive input. Sales is a very tough business. Rejection, prospecting, surprising losses, daily performance pressures, dealing with problems you didn't create in the first place, and maybe even performing for someone you don't respect—all these and many more issues demand a need to "pump yourself up" with positive self-talk.

- I can do this! Look at what I did on this other subject!
- The most professional thing I could do is apologize to ____.
- Now that was a very negative thought! I will never go anywhere with those thoughts.
- Great job on ____. I decided that today that I would make an appointment with so-and-so, and I did! Nice job!
- At least decide on a plan of attack; I shouldn't let this thing fester inside of me one day longer.
- Awesome job on that last call! That was a great question I remembered to ask, and it worked great!

- I have done an awesome job of lining this customer up and eliminating the competition. Now I'll nail it down by doing this _____.
- I *am* making progress! Just look at the last several months. Remember: my original goal was to _____. Don't let my heightened level of success taint the level of celebration as it relates to my original goal.
- Face it; I handled that poorly. I wasn't well prepared, and I should have _____. If I think I will be able to wing these events, I'm wrong.
- My attitude stinks! I'm always negative, my effort has waned, and if I don't get my tail in gear soon, it won't even matter.
- That was the nicest compliment I'm going to get out of my present sales manager. I'm going to look for the positives and hang on to them really tightly and make them last for a while.

You have to be your best cheerleader day in and day out. You can do it! You will step up! You will get your act together! You will win at this game! You will learn from this or that for the rest of your sales career! Now for the last and furthest out there idea: if you want to talk to yourself out loud in the car, put on your cell phone headset or earpiece and talk away. Other drivers won't know whether you are on the phone or talking yourself into heightened success in your job while they drive along listening to their radio!

Be positive, be productive, be strategic! Self-talk away and enjoy the day!

SHOWBOATING IN THE END ZONE

The score is 42–0, and it's late in the game. One team is flying high, and the other team—well, let's say that team can't wait for a hot shower. Then there is Sandy Doss, the high-flying wide receiver, who thinks he's greater than mankind itself. The ball is on the 20-yard line, and Sandy runs his usual post-pattern leaps high into the air and grabs yet another touchdown. The score becomes 48–0. Then to the crowd's amazement, Sandy goes into a showboat routine in the end zone that seems to last forever. He stops short of making a call from his cell phone that is hidden in his sock. All the fans in the stadium roll their eyes in total disgust.

Are you or is someone you know a "Sandy Doss" in the office after a big sale: taking all the credit for the win, talking about how much commission will be paid, letting out yelps, and wallowing in the attention and praise? Well, if you are a "Sandy Doss" in your office, stop, now! These people feel as though it's exactly this bravado that gets them the order in the first place, and they stick with that bravado when they come back to the office. Or they take on the attitude that "without *me*, these people wouldn't have a job!" or "if they wanted to make as much as I do, then they should get into sales like I did!" Take your attitude and shove it! Use all the bravado you think you need to make the sale, but when you come back to the office, dole out the praise. "We got this order because of all of *you*! The presentation packet was perfect! They said they chose us because of the customer service all of *you* provide. The *team* won, and hopefully *we* will make goal because of it."

Great salespeople praise their support staff. They are very careful with gifts for that support staff as well. They realize that the worst thing they can do is make a big commission and buy a couple of cookies for the office. They understand that they don't have to "get" them something; they "give" them something like a personally written thank you note from the heart or a simple beautiful rose.

Truly great salespeople learn to turn their egos on ***and*** off. They turn their greed on ***and*** off. They are truly, genuinely concerned about others instead of just themselves. When the game is over and you look back, make sure you remember how proud you are because of the way you treated others.

If you are not the "Sandy Doss" in your office and you know someone who is, then the best thing to do is copy this chapter and send it to him or her. Maybe make several copies while you're at the copy machine; old habits die hard. It may just take two or three doses of good sense to get through to "Sandy Doss's" thick, dated ego.

OSCARS FOR YOUR SUPPORTING CAST

What's a great salesperson without a supporting cast? Nothing! Early on in your sales career, having someone to help you is probably a long shot at best. In time, however, the more you sell, the higher the chances are of obtaining someone to help or a pool of people to help leverage your time so you can sell more. Why do salespeople have a tendency to burn through their supporting cast? Maybe it's because salespeople have a tendency to be egotistical and rushed for time, and they poorly explain their needs or, worse, don't know what they need. Maybe it's because their requests are unreasonable or don't make any sense. Maybe it's because their tall requests are due to poor planning on their part. Maybe their requests are actually demeaning to the support staff member, not to mention the verbal exchange—or lack thereof—between the two people. Maybe it's just because of the attitude some salespeople carry with them as they move through the office or hand over their needs. Bottom line: great salespeople usually have excellent rapport with their support staff, and it's not because they shower them with gifts all the time or are continually apologizing.

The truly great salespeople level the playing field with their support staff. They start by feeling that everyone is of equal status. It's not an issue of sales production or ego; it's simply an attitude of "Listen: I couldn't do this without you, and I appreciate all the support you offer because it helps me _____." This salesperson asks the support member for a set of parameters to work by day in and day out. They create common ground together, and they respect each other and the lines they have drawn together. They decide on acceptable turnaround time frame expectations. They decide on the amount of information the salesperson is required to offer before the support member spends time on the proposal or presentation packet. The two people truly realize and believe that they need each other and that two are much more powerful than one. Great salespeople also respect their support staff and are willing to accept *and implement* their support staff's suggestions as to how *they* might improve. These great salespeople also tread ever so lightly on any issues of wage, commission, or monetary reward because they are cognizant of the inherent differences in these subjects as they relate to their support staff.

In order to be a truly great salesperson, you must cherish your support staff and be the envy of other support members because they get to work with someone as cooperative as you. If there is friction between the two of you at any given time, which is bound to happen, be proactive and sit down and talk about it sooner rather than later. Accommodate their requests of *you* to change, and make the changes required to keep the relationship firing on all cylinders. The pleasure of working with you should far outweigh the amount of gifts the others give their support staff members for having to put up with them. A nice rose and a personal thank you note sometimes are more than enough if the two of you have created this special bond together. Add in a genuine interest in their personal lives and the joys they cherish in their lives and you will make your life in sales a great deal easier, and you'll sell more!

PARK YOUR OWN TURBO

That's right: you took the commission check from the biggest project ever, and just like you promised, you went out and purchased a brand new Porsche Turbo. No, it's not a lease; it's yours! It's black, it's beautiful, and it's yours, all yours. Since getting it last week, you have been getting your share of exercise walking all those parking lots—because now you always park on the outer edges. This weekend you'll be dropping the rest of the wad at the nicest hotel in Chicago with your significant other. The weekend has arrived, and the two of you climb in for the trip to the Windy City. You are proud of yourself by keeping the car under 70 mph the whole way, using only a quarter of the speedometer dial and leaving the rest for the track. You pull up to the hotel, and the valet attendant is right in your face with his hand out for the keys. You weren't expecting this; let him drive your new Turbo, much less wonder where he parks it? You continue to tightly clutch your keys as you try to forget that annoying smile on his face. Suddenly everyone is way too close to your new car. The bellman moves his metal cart too close; it's windy, and that cart is on wheels. Finally you gather your wits, bags first; you need some time to think. You quickly take a position between the bellman's metal cart and your Turbo. The bags are on his cart, and then you say to your significant other, "I'll be right back. Here's the charge card and $5 for him. I'm going to park my own car!" You look at the valet, tell him to get in the passenger seat, you keep clenching the keys, and get in to drive. "Not only am I driving to the parking garage, but I'm picking out the parking spot!" you say as you drive off. Suddenly that annoying smile on the valet's face is gone, and you're breathing again.

Don't just hand over the keys when you fly or drive in to visit your distributor, dealer, broker, or sales agency. Do *they* park your product line? Do *they* drive your product offering or just parts of it, usually only the best parts? Do *they* take you to *their* clients? Do *you* ever feel as though you are riding in the backseat when you visit? Do *they* drive when you arrive? Or do you say, "Climb in! Here's where we are going today! Together *we* are going to park *my* product line!"

I don't care what car or product line you drive; standing behind someone while he or she talks to *his or her* client, as you try to get a word in edgewise, is very frustrating. It's like this person has created a human shield between you and *his or her* end user. You never seem to get all the information. Decisions are made without a true understanding of how and why they were made. It seems that all the sales meetings and drinks you buy never seem to move the sales figures to where you think they should be. You feel as though you are at a fast food restaurant and the counter service just told you to "step aside."

Whether you sell for the manufacturer or distributor, take a moment to accomplish the following. Obviously, the game is all about the end user. No one owns an end user—no one! Only an end user decides who he or she uses and embraces. It's up to both salespeople on the account to truly create the "team" in teamwork

as it relates to the end user. If ever there is a time for an "open and honest" environment, it is here. The distributor salesperson and the product salesperson must develop a strategy in an open and honest environment that truly pursues particular end users to both people's benefit. Protectionism is "old school" and doesn't work. Sit in a quiet spot together and develop a business plan. Set goals for the account as they relate to the following:

- Discus sales dollars to be expected at the account and the time frame in which those sales dollars should begin to appear.
- Agree on a strategic series of sales contacts at the account as well as who will conduct those contacts.
- Collaborate on where the product line fits at the account and how the two of you will make it happen.
- Assign specific responsibilities at the account; each salesperson has to be accountable for his or her specific responsibilities and time-specific results.
- Mutually agree on the plan and write it down and agree on who should manage the plan.

These business plans by account can then be combined to formulate a business plan for the distributor, dealer, or broker as a whole. The management of this business plan is everyone's responsibility. Oftentimes the manufacturer's salesperson *expects* these items above to just happen. The salesperson could be heard saying, "That's their job; that's why we have hired them to represent us. I'm not going to micro-manage the account! If I micro-managed every account, I might as well sell it all myself!" The business plan concept above is not to be considered "micro-managing"; it should be considered as a requirement to handling any account professionally. Set the framework for success, and get all parties to buy in and manage the process. Even with this framework, it will be tough to become truly satisfied with the outcomes, but without a business plan, the two of you have a minimal chance of success on these individual accounts, and the relationship between the manufacturer and distributor company as a whole will always be strained.

Developing this business plan–based relationship will also provide a good, sound basis for the two of you to part company. If these mutually agreed upon objectives are not being met, then this plan will be the basis for higher-level discussions that may result in a "move" in the marketplace. Remember, however: the grass isn't always greener in the new pasture. Sometimes it looks greener from a distance, but when you actually arrive, it's not what you expected. Each distributor has its own set of frustrations. Make sure this business plan becomes the basis for success at the existing distributor because many times it makes more sense to water the grass you are currently standing on.

Strategically analyze your relationships, develop a business plan as a template for success, and foster common ground. If you are the salesperson for the manufacturer, remember that even though the valet is standing there with his hand out, you still have the right to "park your own Turbo" and choose the parking spot. Be proactive, decide on a strategy, and manage that strategy. Some day you will own a Porsche Turbo!

ORGANIZE AND SUCCEED

THE TANGLED UNDERWEAR AWARD

"And the winner of this year's coveted 'Tangled Underwear Award' is …." Would you be on the short list for this award or worse yet the obvious winner?

All salespeople get tangled up in their underwear from time to time. Family commitments, a peak selling season, or a large project can all affect the number of balls anyone can juggle at any given time. But, some salespeople are tangled up in their underwear most, if not all, of the time. Some can't ever seem to untangle their mess. Certainly, sometimes these people sell more than others, and that's their excuse for always being rushed, hurried, and short with others. Most of the time it relates not so much to actual sales volume but just to unorganized approaches to the hectic everyday life in sales. It's very difficult to get organized in sales for a variety of reasons. Sometimes it relates to the varied locations whereby salespeople have to be productive. At the office, then in the car or plane, back to the office, etc., can be very disruptive and taxing physically at times or all the time. The multitudes of interruptions that occur throughout a day add up, especially when you consider that in sales, everyone's important. Usually salespeople are working through others to make certain things happen by a specific time period, a time period that is usually too short. Add in some substantial ups and downs from winning and losing in sales, and it's difficult to keep it all together sometimes. I offer some suggestions that have helped me over the years, and they may reinforce what you already do or may possibly be of help to some of you.

Getting organized begins for me by getting everything in one spot. I live by my binder, and I take it on every call! Everything important is in my binder. My binder accommodates 8½ by 11 sheets of paper. Most of the information I wanted to track came to me in this format, and it was very easy to place this information in my binder in an acetate sheet protector. Phone directories, discount schedules, pre-call plans, contract guidelines, personal goals and sales goals, commission schedules, my business cards and my clients' business cards—just about anything I referred to frequently or wished I had available but never seemed to actually have when I needed it. I would stop, avoid procrastinating, and specifically place these items in my binder as soon as I thought of them or when they were available. As soon as I open my binder, on the left side of the cover is my calendar. I hated all mass-produced calendars, so I produced my own. Talk about anal! But, I love my calendar. The best part about my calendar is the fact that I know how great or terrible next week will be this week 50% of the time because two weeks are shown on one page. (Exhibit A) Staying on the "everything in one spot" theme, return phone calls, phone numbers, follow-up requirements—everything pertinent is all on my yellow pad in my binder. Any time anyone calls or when I retrieve voice mails or e-mails, anything and everything I need to follow up on later goes on this yellow pad—everything. The pad goes in the binder. My binder also includes an extra supply of business cards so I never run out, my calculator, an architect's scale, and everything else needed to be prepared and look professional in front of the client. It also includes all my prospecting lists, sales reports, territorial maps, and promotions, as well as my sales funnel, etc. Take a good, honest look at the true efficiencies of an electronic system for these items versus a paper system. An electronic system isn't always better just because it's electronic. It has to work and create efficiency. Maybe a combination of an electronic and a paper system works best. The key is to be open-minded and implement the best system for tracking and follow-up possible. If you miss an appointment because of your system or have to get back to someone because of your system or forget to follow up with someone because of your system, then be honest and change your system for the better and be better because of it!

Organize your automobile as well. It's got to have a stapler, paper clips, extra pads of paper, and even more business cards, quote forms, etc.—anything that you have in your non-mobile office. There should almost never be an excuse to have to go back to the office to do something. Ideally, the best salespeople are as productive, if not more productive, in the field as they are at the office. About the only things that draw those salespeople back to the office are those *exciting* sales meetings and the fact that they don't like to prospect new customers on their cell phones. The best are producing a quote for one client on their laptop in their car right before their next face-to-face call with another client. They've eliminated the need to go back to the office for most everything, and they pride themselves in it.

It's important to remember that procrastination sucks the wind out of getting organized. Whenever you see, feel, or hear Mr. Pro Crastination speaking in your mind, stomp on him. Take an immediate time-out and take care of the matter right then and there or write it down. And if you should happen to think of anything for a second time, kick yourself in the butt and write it down on your pad. You'll put your mind and butt at ease.

It's amazing how many people say they need to take the time to get organized! I suppose if you're not organized, then you may never have the time to get organized in the first place. Get off the sales merry-go-round and get on some stable ground and get organized right now! These initial hours you spend now will go a long way toward making available the time in the future to stay organized. So pull off to the side of the road, analyze everything you do, and make it more efficient than it is presently. Analyze all the items you always seem to need but never seem to have with you at the time. Combine all your to-do lists in one list. Define all your prospects to one listing. Work hard to have one of everything important in a binder that is always with you.

Monday _____	**Tuesday** _____	**Wednesday** _____	**Thursday** _____	**Friday** _____
_____	_____	_____	_____	_____
_____	_____	_____	_____	_____
_____	_____	_____	_____	_____
_____	_____	_____	_____	_____
_____	_____	_____	_____	_____
_____	_____	_____	_____	_____
_____	_____	_____	_____	_____
_____	_____	_____	_____	_____
_____	_____	_____	_____	_____
_____	_____	_____	_____	_____
_____	_____	_____	_____	_____
_____	_____	_____	_____	_____
_____	_____	_____	_____	_____

Monday _____	**Tuesday** _____	**Wednesday** _____	**Thursday** _____	**Friday** _____
_____	_____	_____	_____	_____
_____	_____	_____	_____	_____
_____	_____	_____	_____	_____
_____	_____	_____	_____	_____
_____	_____	_____	_____	_____
_____	_____	_____	_____	_____
_____	_____	_____	_____	_____
_____	_____	_____	_____	_____
_____	_____	_____	_____	_____
_____	_____	_____	_____	_____
_____	_____	_____	_____	_____
_____	_____	_____	_____	_____
_____	_____	_____	_____	_____

A SALESPERSON'S WORST NIGHTMARE

It's Monday! Time to go back to work. It's always tough to get going on Mondays. But, finally, you arrive. You wander over to the coffee machine, get your first cup of coffee, chat about the weekend with colleagues, and return to your desk. You open up your binder and take a look at your calendar, and there it is, another week without a single appointment. This just confirms your thoughts from the weekend. Well, you do have lunch with a friend scheduled for Thursday, and you have to be home at 6:00 p.m. on Wednesday. But, that's it; the nightmare has repeated itself. You're ready for another cup of coffee, and it's time to get up anyway—anything to escape from another blank schedule for the week.

How do you stop this vicious cycle? Obviously, the goal would be to think about next week when it's this week. But, it's hard! The days always seem to run together, and the current week consumes all your energy and planning, so you convince yourself to just think about next week—well—next week! **Take out your calendar right now!** I'll wait here. OK! For the next eight weeks, cross out a morning or an afternoon whenever you are at your best in each week, preferably the same weekday each week so as to develop a routine. OK, you just crossed off four hours of time each week for the next eight weeks. That time is to be labeled "**proactive time**." Nothing else happens during proactive time except the time spent to call, coordinate, and set appointments for future days or weeks. No other phone calls, no interruptions, no unexpected anythings, just you, the phone, and your "**proactive list**." The proactive list is a yellow pad with all the names and phone numbers that represent future opportunities for you. Leads, opportunities, index cards with your projects, and anything you use to track future possibilities for appointments. Now the tough part: sit down for the next four hours and just call and set a goal for how many appointments you will set to achieve success—and then set them. At the end of the four hours, evaluate yourself on how many appointments you actually made versus your goal. Before next week, during "non-peak" hours, revise and review your proactive list so you are ready to be productive right out of the gates next week when you do it again. This concentrated proactive effort along with ongoing efforts you pursue during each week should fill up future weeks to a much greater extent. If not, do some revising, but always remember to cross out proactive time on your schedule each and every week without exception!

The best salespeople have next week well in hand by the end of this week. They have allocated the time to be proactive during the current week without totally shutting down their entire operation for days at a time to do so. The best also leverage their time by using a telechannel support person if one is available to them. Sometimes companies make available people to assist in the development of leads or actually set appointments for the salesperson. Embrace these people and give them specific tasks that *augment* your attack. These tasks could be making appointments with very hard to reach prospects. Have *them* make the 20 calls for you and give *them* the times when you could meet or some times an appointment with so-and-so would take precedence over anything else. Give *them* a list of questions you would like for *them* to ask to qualify a potential lead under *your terms*. Eliminate going on another call that they set up without your established pre-call parameters being qualified in advance. Or don't let them set up the appointment; just let them get the information for your review. Fully utilize these people, but give them guidance as to what you want so you create the powerful connection and positive results. This assistance is not a replacement for your own proactive list attack. It *augments* the program we agreed upon above. The best salespeople still do most of their own prospecting because they realize that they are the best at perceiving potential and they want to be on the front lines when it comes to prospecting and the income they will or will not make in the future.

CHINESE FIRE DRILL

"I'll have that for you tomorrow!" "I'll bring that proposal to you in two days!" "Heck, I've got the time to do that today!" "I'll work on that this weekend and have it for you first thing Monday morning!" "I want to be the first proposal you receive, so I'll have it by Thursday!" After a whole month of these aggressive promises, this salesperson will have created a "Chinese fire drill" for himself or herself. He or she will rush around trying to meet self-imposed, aggressively set deadlines. Then this salesperson will push his or her support staff to meet those deadlines regardless of any other priorities. He or she will forget to allow time for problems or possible delays in obtaining all the required information. Add in a heightened chance for mistakes, oversights, unprofessional proposals, not to mention the possibility of missing these self-imposed deadlines, and this salesperson is mixing a recipe for failure, burnout, or both!

"When would *you* like for me to respond?" "Is next Thursday OK?" "Would late Monday be OK?" The best salespeople let the customer decide on the time frame for reporting back. Most of the time this leaves enough time for possible delays and unknown problems and time to recheck for any mistakes and, most important, time for the support staff to accommodate the request into *their* schedule. If the time frame the salesperson suggests is not acceptable, the client will say so! No one will be offended, and a readjustment of the time frame will follow. These salespeople avoid the pitfalls in the paragraph above and operate under what I call "deadline control." They always seem like such "cool operators." Their support staff loves them, and these staff members also realize that when a rushed deadline is imposed, the salesperson most likely had no choice in the situation. Additionally, these salespeople end up making fewer mistakes and excuses like "I'm sorry I forgot to _____" or "I wasn't able to _____" or "I'm sorry about that pricing error" or "I just didn't have time to _____." Additionally, their clients perceive this "cool under pressure" nature to be a real positive and one the clients may need to rely on later when the chips are down. Or maybe it's just the fact that clients see this salesperson as simply more professional and making fewer mistakes and therefore the risk of using them versus the rushed, flustered salesperson is far less.

Never self-impose a deadline. Let the clients decide on the deadline that's most appropriate for their situation, and make it happen by that deadline every time it's set.

TIME-OUT

If you're a parent with kids over the age of two, you most likely are familiar with the concept of time-outs. If you are soon to be a parent, it won't be long before time-outs become a part of your vocabulary. And if you're still single, most likely a time-out is something a coach or player calls in a sporting event. It doesn't matter when a time-out is called; it's always a time to regroup, review a current or future strategy, or catch a long-awaited deep breath. Or it's simply a time to stop Mr. Mo Mentum from gaining a foothold for the wrong team. Usually after a time-out, a renewed spirit takes hold, whether it's in the form of a child who has been able to calm down or a parent with regained control or a sports team that takes a new, refreshed focus as the team members move forward together.

Salespeople need to take time-outs as part of their daily routine. The constant pressure to perform day in and day out each and every month of every year is relentless. At this point in time, many sales managers would say, "And that's exactly what they are paid to do!" Well, these sales managers might be right, but it doesn't solve the problem. There is still the same constant pressure to meet their sales quotas every day. If you add in the pressure of a little non-performance that all sales people experience at one time or another or the pressure of having to talk to people at a status level of discomfort or a string of recent losses or a manufacturer going through a series of non-performance issues of its own, not to mention all the possible pressures at home, it's no wonder a time-out can be a salesperson's best friend sometimes.

Salespeople must find a favorite *quiet spot or spots* to refresh their spirit, drive, and determination or simply to catch up. I'm so sick of hearing the analogy of "sharpening the saw," but here goes: the best salespeople take the time-out to sharpen their saws even though their competition is still sawing, most likely with a dull blade. Anyway, find this quiet spot and shut everything off. This quiet spot could be the office; ideally, it's not, but if it is the office, it's either early in the morning or late at night. I personally never liked the office as my quiet spot because invariably I would get interrupted and get less accomplished than I expected, except maybe on Saturday or Sunday mornings. Regardless, I needed a quiet spot during business hours as well. So, I would find some great spots that I enjoyed and where I could produce aggressively day in and day out. *I associate great salespeople with a high-paid juggler—a juggler who is paid based on the number of balls he or she can keep juggling without letting any of them drop to the ground.* Embrace these time-outs as a time to keep your present number of balls in the air and strategize how to get even a couple more balls into the mix. Some salespeople use these quiet spots to hide or escape from reality, or they use these spots to become less productive that day and possibly the next day. If you use your quiet spots for these means, there's something wrong. Either the sales profession is not for you or other subjects have clouded your view of the future. It's important to talk to someone about these feelings and get them out on the table for the sake of everyone in your life.

Great uses for your quiet spot:

- A time to bolster your spirits after a couple of losses or even one particular loss.
- Self-talk about even greater production.
- Spend the entire time focusing on the future; develop or refine your proactive list of names and phone numbers on a separate pad of paper that you can refer on the fly in order to keep your funnel full.
- Review your sales numbers as they relate to your quotas.
- Develop your own tracking system and personal reward system.
- Take the time to actually accomplish the item(s) that you have procrastinated about long enough.
- Take the time to embrace the "everything in one spot" theme and transfer all the little notes and reminders you have all over the place to one pad of paper.
- Transfer notes or items for the sole purpose of eliminating pieces of paper or totally organize your current pieces of paper into defined packets.
- Write a couple of hand-written thank you notes instead of being like your competition and sending a quick thanks by e-mail.
- Write down all the "I should do's" that crop into your mind all the time or just do it on an ongoing basis on your to-do list pad.
- Quote or check acknowledgments for errors *before* the items physically appear at your client's doorstep and the problem-solving clock starts ticking away aimlessly and unproductively.

- Read a good book on how to improve in sales. Usually this time is best spent during off-peak hours, but if your off-peak hours are truly committed, read the book during peak hours because it's important to read about your profession.
- Read all those articles your sales manger deems important and really absorb them because there will be a test!

However you decide to utilize your time-outs is up to you, but use the time to get back in the game refreshed, organized, and ready for life in sales with a positive attitude associated with producing results.

TOP 75/ TOP 30

We've all seen the nighttime heat-sensitive photographic shots taken from police helicopters where the camera clearly defines the suspect and where he or she is headed. Wouldn't it be great to fly over your territory with the same type of camera and highlight all the "hot spots" where clients are currently purchasing or deciding to purchase your types of products? If only it were that easy! It takes time to find customers. Many times we have leads and opportunities, but turning those leads and opportunities into our customers is a long and complicated story.

Take the time before you attack a territory to define a "**top 75.**" This is a list of 75 prospects that could be in the market for your products or that could influence the purchasing of your products. Go to your local library, or use the Internet, past sales records, and local listings of top companies in your territory. If you pursue this subject, the lists will begin to appear quickly and so will your ability to get close to a top 75. Really analyze this list and make sure it's in line with your focus. Make sure to place the largest and the smallest prospects on the list. Be careful not to eliminate any prospect just because it is purchasing from someone else or has had

TOP 75

Rep:

	Account Name			Date of Contacts							Sales Volume		
											2005	2006	2007
1													
2													
3													
4													
5													
6													
7													
8													
9													
10													
11													
12													
13													
14													
15													
16													
17													
18													
19													
20													
21													
22													
23													
24													
25													
26													
27													
28													
29													
30													
31													
32													
33													
34													
35													
36													
37													

TOP 75

Rep:

	Account Name			Date of Contacts							Sales Volume		
											2005	2006	2007
38													
39													
40													
41													
42													
43													
44													
45													
46													
47													
48													
49													
50													
51													
52													
53													
54													
55													
56													
57													
58													
59													
60													
61													
62													
63													
64													
65													
66													
67													
68													
69													
70													
71													
72													
73													
74													
75													

a bad experience with your company years ago. Develop a form to accommodate these prospects and the critical parameters for staying on the list. Then attack this list systematically. Proactively call each prospect and find out through pre-formed thought-probing questions whether it is worth an appointment.Even the slightest interest or desire is worth a great deal at this point. Avoid eliminating prospects on your top 75 by a quick "I told you so" to yourself just because you're afraid to develop them because of their size, etc. The key here is to plan and organize your attack before you attack. Believe in your attack. Set a time frame for attacking a certain number of these prospects by a certain date or quarter. Be persistent in your attack and take a "never say die" attitude with you every day you attack. Over time you'll have to revise your list and take some accounts off and replace them with other accounts or other entire markets of new penetration. *How many times do you try an account before you take it off the list? When you decide on the number of times at a particular account, go at least one more time or maybe try two more ideas before you quit. Premature quitting is never a good thing. Always second-guess yourself before you pull that trigger too soon.*

This top 75 evolves over time to a "**top 30**." I like to describe this top 30 list as those **clients** who would rather purchase from you than anyone else. **This is a list of names of *people,* not names of accounts.** These *people* love to invite *you* to their purchasing events. They want to give *you* the business because they like *you* best. These are the *people* who "pull" you through each and every year. They continually call you to come over to their purchasing parties and help them decide! You know who these people are because you have them. The question is, Do you have 30 of them? Start by writing down the ones you do have on your top 30 list and get a list started. Maybe write them all a personal thank you note for their business while you finally have them all on one list,

TOP 30

	Client Name	Company	Phone	Sales Volume		
				2005	2006	2007
1						
2						
3						
4						
5						
6						
7						
8						
9						
10						
11						
12						
13						
14						
15						
16						
17						
18						
19						
20						
21						
22						
23						
24						
25						
26						
27						
28						
29						
30						

somewhat like a christening of your top 30 list! Then commit yourself to cherish and service them with everything you have till the day you quit or they move on to another job. Keep adding names to this list and kick yourself in the butt if *you* ever had anything to do with taking them off the list. Also remember that nobody stays on the list forever no matter how much he or she is currently purchasing. I know it's hard to believe during any current sales frenzy, but everyone's well dries up or the competition starts to drain the well instead of you. Anything can happen and will happen. Always be searching for a replacement—always—but again cherish all of them every day of every week they are in your camp and on your top 30 list.

Every industry is different and so are the numbers associated with these lists. The point is to define these lists so your attack takes a true focus and stays in focus. Maintaining these lists becomes the basis for this focus and your success!

THE BLACK BOX

One of my sales representatives called his laptop the "boat anchor." One of them called it the "black box." Regardless of the special name you associate with your laptop, it's a very special instrument, isn't it? It allows you to get up to 100+ e-mails each day, 20 of which are actually important to doing business. It allows you to check on any customer while you are in your car right before you actually visit with him or her. It allows you to search anonymously on your competitor's Web site to see what the heck an XYZ is and what it looks like. It allows your customers to follow up with you as they sit at their computers all day and every day of the week while you sit in front of your windshield or in an airplane most of each day. And today it even allows you to bid with 50 other vendors without even having to show up at the customer's place of business! The black box has changed a great deal of what salespeople can accomplish in any given day or week or year. The real question is whether it has changed accomplishments in sales for the better or for the worse. I believe the answer is a little of both.

A salesperson certainly can't be face to face with a customer when he or she is checking or replying to e-mails. A salesperson certainly can't be face to face with a customer when he or she is developing the next PowerPoint presentation or Excel spreadsheet. The real question is, since you received your black box, have you sold more or less with it, and are you spending the same time or *more time* in front of customers (face time) as you did before receiving it? I'll make a very bold statement: *every minute of prime-time hours (8 a.m.–5 p.m. weekdays) you are banging away on your black box, be very critical of the use of your time! Most anything you can accomplish on your black box can be accomplished during off-peak hours. Don't let the black box effect the time you spend face to face with your customers! True friendship with your customers is not developed electronically; it's developed personally. A true understanding of how your client feels about you or your solution is not best perceived electronically but personally. The black box should never be an excuse or remedy for not arriving personally. The real power of this technical advantage is to fully utilize both facets, personal visits with electronic follow-up. There seem to be all sorts of reasons why salespeople are face to face with their customers only 30% of the allowable time available to them. The black box is just one more on an already long list of excuses. The best advantage to the black box is that it can be just as powerful during off-peak hours as peak hours!*

Isn't it amazing how time flies when you're "working" on your black box? I remember one of my sales representatives spending all morning (peak hours) coming up with his "**top 75**". He was a marginal performer at best but a wiz at his black box. About 11:30 a.m., he popped his head in my office with a "Got a minute?" I replied sincerely, "Absolutely! Anything for you, Jeff!" Jeff went on to say, "I want to show you my spreadsheet with my top 75 list you required all of us to forward to you." "Jeff, this is very nicely done.

It's the nicest one I've received so far," I said. Jeff eagerly said, "Well, I spent all morning on it. Do you have Michelle's yet?" Michelle was my star. She was the one who sold the most of all the sales representatives on my staff. "In fact I do!" I said as I reached into my folder. I handed Jeff a copy of Michelle's top 75, and it looked like she wrote it while she was driving. Knowing Michelle, she probably wrote it while she was driving to her tenth call of the day! Jeff looked at it in disillusionment, and after a while he said, "This isn't very—well, she must have been really busy when—" The point in all this is that "working" on the black box doesn't necessarily mean that a salesperson is "producing sales" on the black box!

Your black box, or laptop, is, first and foremost, a tool to produce more SALES. Use it during off-peak hours and embrace all of the advantages it offers to help you SELL MORE during peak hours.

DRIVEN, BUT WHERE ARE YOU DRIVING?

What does it mean when people label a person as driven? Where does someone drive when he or she is driven? Are all driven people workaholics? People tagged as "driven" seem well regarded; how do I get some of this "driven" so I can be well regarded? Many people would consider driven people as not necessarily happy people, so what's so good about being driven?

Let's first define "driven." ***In my opinion, someone who is driven has a high level of energy focused toward accomplishing a particular task or tasks over a given length of time.***

Let's look at the variables in the sentence above. The "**level of energy**" a person places toward a task is certainly a variable. Different people have different levels of energy. I'm not sure whether a sales manager can change a person's level of energy to a great extent. Certainly a bigger carrot, like commission or a bonus, tries to address this subject. However, the level of energy someone has is largely innate or built inside. External forces can modify a person's level of energy to an extent but not for an extended period of time. Certainly if one is passionate about something, then the level of energy increases. Are you passionate about the sales profession? To what extent does this level of passion drive you toward success? If the sales profession doesn't create intrigue in your core, then most likely the level of success you achieve will be directly related. For every day you are in sales, continue to develop a level of passion for sales inside of you that spurs on your level of energy to succeed. Be driven to succeed at the beginning of your sales career, and keep building more and more success throughout your career in sales.

The next part of the sentence above is "**focused**." Many people have lots of drive, but they can't focus that drive in a particular direction for the time it takes to succeed. They scatter their energy in many directions, and it becomes diluted. First, sit in a quiet spot and decide which short-range tasks are required to reach an important goal, and then take that level of energy and determination you have and focus it toward those tasks. Finish those tasks and the overall goal with the focus of a laser beam and move to the next goal. It sounds so simple, but for many salespeople, it's not, and it's not due to a lack of overall effort. It's due to a lack of overall sustained focus to **and** through the finish line!

The art of "**accomplishing a task**" seems so simple until you try it day in and day out in sales. Life in sales is a flurry of activity, and sooner rather than later, a new task seems like a priority or we lose energy toward the original task for a variety of reasons such as the rejection we might receive. Make your list, develop your plan, set a target, and make it happen. Salespeople have the best intentions—for a while. They charge ahead with great abandon, and then they run out of steam or change course. Stay the course! Apply an entire week if you deemed it important to obtaining the sale and get it done.

The last concept in the sentence above is "**a given length of time**." Always apply a time line to your goals. The tasks you deem necessary to achieve your goals must have a defined time line. This time line must be adhered to and followed so that new goals can be put in place as new priorities after the old ones have been accomplished. Celebrate accomplishment of goals by taking the time to cherish the achievement either by yourself or with someone special.

Salespeople must decide on goals that are productive. Oftentimes in sales, time is of the essence. There isn't much time to decide on a goal that isn't productive in the foreseeable future. Strategically decide on your goals because of their immediate productivity toward the overall objective, retaining your job through performance. Decide on goals that are the most a tune to hitting this target, keeping your job. Some salespeople decide on goals that would be nice or that are not an integral part to a larger picture, and they waste valuable time pursuing them and end up with a blank sheet at the end. Every day counts, and every minute of every hour counts as it relates to reaching strategic goals. Develop a sense of urgency in achieving every task that adds up to achieving every goal and never forget the ultimate goal of all goals, **SELLING MORE THAN BEFORE!**

Are driven people workaholics? Some are, but many are not. Workaholics get this label because they don't leave enough time for others in their lives or themselves for that matter. It's important to decide how many hours you will work each week to be successful and still have enough time for family or yourself. Regard the time you spend with your family as just as important as the time you spend at work. Decide specifically which hours you will work each week, stick to those specific hours each week, and don't go over, except on rare occasions. Keeping this regiment is very important as long as it allows enough time for family. Many salespeople don't utilize every allowable minute when they are working to the best of their advantage, and they keep drifting over to family time. It's not acceptable, and **they need to be more efficient during peak hours**. When it is truly family time, that's exactly what it is—no cell phone interruptions, no "Oh, I forgot to _____." Decide to work

6:00 a.m. to 6:00 p.m. every day and from 6:00 to 10:00 a.m. on Saturdays, and don't change it for anything. Your world without your family could be worse than anything. Cherish them, nurture them, and make sure when it's all over and you're on the beach walking, they're walking right beside you. Don't lose them because you worked too hard. It will be a very hollow victory in the end.

You can't go to Best Buy and purchase some "driven" for yourself. There are some things you can do to create more drive in your life, however, and one of them is to get in shape. If you are out of shape, you'll run out of gas every day at 3:30 p.m. or earlier! Run through the finish line every day, and the finish line is that last call each day at 4:00 p.m. Those last calls really add up, and a whole year of them—well—they will make the year! If you're out of shape or have lost your passion or drive to succeed, that last call drops by the wayside more times than not. Don't let it! Suck it up, and kick yourself in the butt for driving home early before making that last call at 4:00 p.m. Get yourself in shape mentally and physically to make that call and make it productive.

Can driven people actually be happy? All people are hopefully happy when they get to their destination. It's important for people who are driven to have a destination! It starts with sitting down and setting realistic targets for personal happiness. Write these targets down, keep them in your binder, and look at them on occasion. Don't keep extending them as time passes. Begin to become happier and happier the closer you get to achieving your goals. Usually, driven people get close to achieving their goals, but they have a tough time being happy about it because as soon as they get close, they always want more. Begin to lose your yearning to always want more as soon as you get close to your original goal. Acquire the original goal and settle down a little, smile, smell some roses, and truly begin to cherish others around you. It won't be the last goal you will ever set. Take the time to be happy with your achievement.

The buzz today among sales managers is how much they hate complacency. Salespeople who are happy with life and their income level are at peace with what they have accomplished and really don't need any more. The sales manager is never happy with status quo or complacency. If you are happy with where you are in life and are not driven to exceed, trouble is in your future. These two concepts don't mix. Salespeople can never feel complacent or else a good sales manager will have them staring at the exit door sooner than they think. Push complacency aside until you are retired. Run through the finish line in your career!

Get out your map, start driving, and reach your destinations. At the end, make sure you smell the roses with your closest supporters!

SHAKEN, NOT STIRRED

The big order came in today. The fish is in the boat. Ring the bell. "Honey, it's time for that trip with the kids! Book it! I'm going to stop and celebrate on the way home, and I'll be home at the usual time, 6:00 p.m."

The bartender sets up your spot at the bar. *This* time you are going to take the time to celebrate. A little time alone on your own, with one favorite martini, straight up, shaken, not stirred, at the best spot in town for martinis. It's a beautiful spot; the bartender puts down a white placemat with a nice "real" cloth napkin and slowly pours the clear, chilled martini into a tall wide-mouthed glass. As a last final touch, two nice, large, blue cheese-stuffed olives sit down near the bottom. You cherish this moment for a time and think back to all the hoops you had to jump through to get this one. As you take your first sip, you cherish the thought that your competition is depressed right about now and is wondering what went wrong or worse what sneaky move you pulled at the end to take it. Your competition is probably talking about how you "gave" it away, when in actuality you still had room to go in price. *You had the relationships, you created value, you had all the information, and in fact, it wasn't about price at all!* You take another sip. At $2.00 a sip, you decide to sip very slowly. There's no rush, anyway; it's just you and your win. You decide to write a nice thank you note to your support staff and bring them each a rose tomorrow. As you look down again and stare at the martini glass, the glass reminds you of something. You can't put your finger on it right away, but then it dawns on you: *this is a picture of your current sales funnel.* Oh, relax, Scott! Cherish your win! Now is not the time to think about your sales funnel! Don't ruin this wonderful event. You're sick! You can't even take a moment to cherish your last big win, and you're already worried about your sales funnel. Sure enough, you don't have many prospects in the top of the funnel. You have spent so much time getting the "big one" that you haven't even thought about loading the top of your funnel. It's not like you have finished the martini and your funnel is dry. You still have projects in the middle of the funnel or glass. And those two large projects that are ready to drop through the bottom of the funnel are still there. You haven't eaten the olives yet! Give yourself a break! OK, tomorrow you will begin to fill the top of the funnel. Before work tomorrow, you will go over your proactive list and take a look at all the leads you have clipped over time and formulate your future. You take another $2.00 sip, and it tastes better than the last sip. Now, you are back on track! Enjoy this moment, cherish your awesome win, smell the roses, and get back at it early tomorrow. **You realize that everyone is right; you are obsessed with sales. You love it! You have found your niche! It feels great! The last sips go down really smoothly, and tonight, you feel just like James Bond!**

A TIME TO MOVE ON

IT'S EASIER TO FAIL IN SALES THAN YOU THINK

Many people look at salespeople, especially successful salespeople, and say, "If they can sell, I certainly can sell. I can't believe they make that much money for what they do! That is, when they are not playing golf! With our great products, anyone could sell them!" Talk is certainly cheap. Until you're successfully in the sales profession for several years, sales is easier said than done.

Let's analyze why it's so easy to fail in sales. Let's say no one liked you when you came in for an appointment. You had an air about you that was difficult to stand for very long. Or after the meeting, you said you would follow up and then didn't write down the items for follow-up and forgot to follow up on any or some of them. Or let's say after the meeting, you wrote up the proposal but added wrong and the quote was $10,000 short. Let's say that you procrastinated on the quote for five weeks and finally sent the quote to the prospect a month late. Let's say when you got back in your car, you misplaced the notes you took during the meeting and couldn't find them and really had no idea what you needed to follow up on at all. Let's say during the meeting you just talked and talked and the meeting became all about you!

Let's say your most favorite prospect, your closest buddy so far in sales, has been quoted on 20 different occasions and hasn't purchased one item from you. In fact, today the two of you are going to lunch together and you'll try to find a way to ask him about it, but when it gets to be time, you never have has the guts to say anything. You vowed to yourself when you took the job in sales that you would never become a pushy salesperson. Let's say that your sales manager always thinks of a strategy for the next step at your accounts that is different from what you would try to accomplish. He never seems to know your account like you do, and if he did, he would understand why his strategy wouldn't work at this particular account. Let's say you were always 15–30 minutes late. Let's say that every time you try to listen to the client, you find yourself daydreaming on another subject and find it really difficult to be intrigued by what he or she has to say. It's just going to be all about the price anyway, so all this other stuff is just something to do to fill up the time before you show the price. Let's say you hate to get up every morning knowing you have to generate something today, every day, every week, every month and be happy about it to everyone around you. Enough said! We could go on and on about failing in sales. The fact of the matter is that sales is a very tough profession. It's even tougher to be successful at it!

This book is certainly not about failing in sales—just the opposite in fact. It is about understanding what it takes to become successful in sales. Take a close look at the sentences above one by one. Certainly there are different degrees to which they might be true in your everyday sales activities. Use this book to make yourself aware of these and other pitfalls in sales that even the best have to work on every day. Also use this book to privately decide whether the sales profession is for you. The next time someone starts to compare income levels and talks about how easy it must be to be in sales, just stand tall and proud about your accomplishments in the sales profession. That person can get into sales anytime he or she wants, just like you did years ago. Until that person is also successful at sales like you are, talk is cheap!

HOW MANY SHARKS SWIM IN YOUR TANK?

We've all read about shark attacks on our beaches. We've seen shots of sharks attacking a diver in a steel cage. Most of us have been to an aquarium or two and have seen sharks swim around like they own the place. In business, sometimes sharks *do* own the place. They seem nice enough during the interview process, but then again, you're with them only a short time. When there's a shark in the area, things are simply tense. Everyone is cautious, calculating, always on the lookout, and concerned about who is swimming behind him or her. Quite honestly, most of the time, it is not a very spontaneous, creative, risk-taking environment, and it is certainly not open and honest. If you're not good at swimming with a shark or for that matter several sharks, then you have to be on your guard most of the time. The best way to ward off the shark or sharks in sales is to perform. Selling a great deal is usually the antidote for survival. Remaining quiet when the sharks are present also helps—just keep your mouth shut. That is, until you are asked for your opinion. When your chance to speak occurs, hopefully you have planned ahead. Open your binder and write in a section what you will say when it's time to have that most important encounter. Plan ahead and write down your thoughts, and when asked, talk in a clear, concise, positive manner. Also remember to talk about what you have produced, what you will produce soon, and how dedicated you are to the company. *If it's your time to speak and you have no opinion or you react with silence, you've missed a chance to make a positive impression of your abilities or, worse, you've created a negative impression of your abilities. Remember, sharks move fast and form opinions fast! Great salespeople write down what they will say when it's time, and they are mentally prepared for the event ahead. They flip to the appropriate section of their binder, and they talk in specifics and performance-based facts and goals.*

Many times the shark bites, the blood is in the water, and you're a marked mammal. Usually either you are allowed to swim in their tank or they want you to leave the tank sooner rather than later. Life in the tank may never be the same again. Maybe there is a rock to hide behind, but usually life is too short to be hiding behind rocks for the rest of your career. Stick around for a while to see how bad the bite is and whether it will heal, or begin to look for a different tank. As you seek other tanks, do as much checking as you can to seek out the sharks ahead of time. Don't be naive; the sea is full of sharks, and it's important to find a tank that is virtually free of them. You will find a tank free of sharks, and swimming in those tanks will be a true pleasure for many years to come.

Salespeople who believe they have to be tough sharks themselves to survive may survive for a while, but there's always tougher sharks out there, and tough sharks love a fight. Over time, you will lose. Never be a shark with your customers, or you will lose even quicker. Try to be one of those big fish in the tank that moves around the tank quietly and just produces year after year and cherishes the good parts about the tank.

May your swim in sales always be free of sharks, or over time, may you just learn to swim in the opposite direction. Do yourself, your family, and your career a favor by not hiding behind the rocks for very long when big sharks own the tank and have a vicious bite.

FLYING ABOVE THE CLOUDS

Most of us have flown in some lousy weather over the years. It's the type of weather when you drive to the airport and try to judge how far you can see on the ground much less in the air. When you hear that the plane is scheduled to depart, you seem happy, but deep down you wonder whether you'll make it. The plane taxis down the runway, and soon you're in the air and on your way. You look out the window into total gray. The gray lasts for what seems to be an eternity. Then, finally, the gray seems to begin to break up a little, and before you know it, the plane ascends above the clouds, and the gray a minute ago turns to a bright blue. All of a sudden you can see for miles, and the sky is the brightest blue that can be imagined, and the sun just glistens off the tops of the clouds. What a dramatic transformation in just a matter of seconds.

Turmoil in the sales profession can be the same way. At times for days or even months, your life in sales seems like the most solid gray packed-tight weather formation you have ever experienced. Sometimes it's a political problem inside the office that just doesn't seem to clear up. Sometimes it's the lack of sales performance to your goal. Sometimes it's an extended losing streak that doesn't seem to pass. Sometimes it's all the balls we juggle for ourselves *and* everyone else. Whatever the reason for the depressing situation, at times it seems like the solid gray will never clear up. Just remember that all things pass—all things! First and foremost, be patient, calm, and professional, and don't lose your cool. Strap yourself in and wait out the current storm. As long as your plane is on an ascent, sooner or later it will break through the clouds; it's just a matter of time. If your situation isn't on a path of ascent, you might just stay in the clouds much longer than what is personally tolerable. In that case, take an inventory of what *you* can change to make the situation better and at least get your plane ascending! Pick two things *you* could begin to do differently and commit to them. It could be telling someone you're sorry; acknowledge the situation and explain to this person the commitment you have made to make these two changes. Always take some action you deem to be a positive step forward. Try to see the other side of the picture or make a compromise—anything that would help get your plane ascending above the clouds. It's important to put your stubbornness aside and be open and honest about the situation with all involved and move above the clouds. Sales is a difficult profession, even without having to add in all sorts of extra turmoil. Clear it up, take a professional, unselfish approach, and solve it. The longer the frustration festers, the worse the toll will be on your customers, your family, and yourself. It's really not worth it in the long run. The anxiety associated with hanging onto the principle of it is far more detrimental than compromising and moving on. Rise above the clouds and check out the blue skies that will appear after the turmoil is behind you, not to mention the warmth of the sun.

Sometimes no matter what you *honestly* do to try to change *your* approach to turmoil, the situation remains the same. As long as you are honest with yourself and *you* have put your stubbornness aside and have sincerely tried to change, then the rest of the chapters in this section become more appropriate. Be ready, however, for even more turmoil that comes with any job change, including its effect on your résumé. If this same situation has presented itself before in your career, maybe it's time for some reflection on sales as a career for you and time for you to seek advice from an informed, independent experienced salesperson for an objective opinion of the situation.

Remember: if you want to put the solid gray skies behind you, you have to start the process by changing, and then you have to get your plane on a path of ascent. Once you have taken the initiative, have become professional about the situation, and have started the process of change, then blue skies are in your future!

POLISHING PLAN B

Remaining at the same job for many years is an exception, not the rule, in today's business environment. Turnover in the sales profession has always been higher than the norm, and today, it's probably even higher. As today's fast-paced sales environment consumes all your energy, it's easy to forget about good old Plan B. Obviously this is the employment strategy you quickly shift into when your current strategy begins to fail. It's always important to polish Plan B and keep it shinny. Without continued thought, Plan B will become tarnished, and it won't be polished up when you need it most. Plan B is important for all salespeople but especially for those salespeople living on the outer edge of their means. As your financial obligations build and your family grows, Plan B becomes even more important. The rainy-day nest egg will be consumed very quickly, and the reality of change in lifestyle will hit sooner rather than later.

Sometimes Plan B can be an entrepreneurial leap, like starting your own game in the sales profession. It takes time, hard work, great planning, high finance, and guts to make this leap. If you have been successful in everything you have encountered in sales, then the odds are with you. However, odds are still odds and not a guarantee of success. Entrepreneurs possess many quality traits, some of which will be brand new to you and untested. Some polish Plan B and meet the test with flying colors and never look back. Others, well, they get an A for effort and fall back under someone else's umbrella during a future storm. Regardless of whether it's a long-awaited entrepreneurial venture or simply moving on to another tank to swim, keeping Plan B polished is critical. You will always hold the personal reward for making this successful change in your career high, and your chances of success will be much higher with a well-thought-out Plan B. Remember that the employment race is a long race, probably 40 years. Most likely, Plan B will be used several times in a great career. Constantly keep revising your Plan B, and look forward to implementation at particular points in your career. When it's time to walk on the beach, when it's all over, cherish the fact that you followed your dream to the best of your abilities. Then *take in* all the satisfaction associated your well-planned, strategic journey!

THE WRITING IS ON THE WALL

"The writing is on the wall!" "No it's not; there is no writing on the wall." "Yes, the writing, well, it's on the wall!" "The writing can't be on the wall." "I saw the writing with my own eyes, and it's on the wall all right!" "OK, maybe the writing is on the wall, but it's not *my* writing that is on the wall." "I'm sorry; I saw the writing, and yes, it's *your* writing that is on the wall." "I don't believe you; it can't be." "I'll show you! I'll take you to the writing—*your* writing that is on the wall." "OK, I have to see for myself. You have to be wrong, dead wrong." "Well, here we are! You'll have to open your eyes if you want to find out whether it's your writing on the wall." "OK, just give me a minute. I'm ready! My eyes are open now. You're right! It's my writing on the wall. I can't believe it. I have given this job my all!"

Adversity and the end are tough to see clearly for a while. We all have a difficult time understanding all the reasons why we are cast aside at points in our sales careers. First and foremost, react professionally when you realize your writing is on the wall. Remain quiet, calm, calculating, and in control no matter how difficult or blindsided you might feel at the time. Get yourself into a quiet spot as soon as you can after the situation has presented itself, ideally away from the scene and alone. Try to bring clarity to the situation, replay the cards in your mind, and begin to structure your future. That last sentence is much easier said than done, of course. It may take months to actually accomplish all of the steps in that sentence. The main point is that you get to the "structure your future" phase. Also make a point to minimize negative criticism of all the people involved no matter how difficult it may be at the time. Salespeople handle rejection all the time, but this type of rejection hits right to the core of one's being. This is the time to reach down deep and hang onto your core for dear life. Get some tapes to help you through. Try to talk to friends about the situation in as positive a light as possible.

Hopefully, these core beliefs we have been talking about are solid as a rock, full of determination, confidence, and persistence, and tap your belief that there is a plan for your life *and* career. Someone else could be the real judge as to where your career should be headed. Follow your instincts, and the right path will appear. Sometimes adversity is just what each one of us needs to grow and more fully enjoy the plan that lies ahead. It's natural to waver during this time of challenge, but find stable ground, stand up, brush yourself off, and vow to bring value to someone else, someone who appreciates it. Focus on the future; time spent thinking about the past is unproductive. Move on, stay positive, and immediately work hard to understand and embrace this much-needed change in your career. Embrace new opportunity when it appears; analyze it, but don't rush into it. If it continues to feel right after several days in a row, then begin the next chapter in your career and work your tail off to make it a successful chapter. You have a great deal of value to give some company that appreciates it, so give it everything you've got to offer.

How many times have we heard the phrase "learn from your mistakes"? Are you able to embrace this concept, or are you above it? Some salespeople never think it's their fault. They are quick to blame everyone else but themselves. Not everyone else is to blame. Part of reaching down deep to your core involves thinking back to about what *you* could have done differently, what *you* need to change to make *your* future brighter. The minute we place ourselves above *our* need to change is the day our days will not be as bright as they could be if we would only point the arrow at ourselves and embrace true change. The reason *your* writing is on the wall is because *you* did something wrong. Face the facts and use the experience to change something about *you* for the better.

> *I certainly have first-hand experience with this subject—just as you might. So many salespeople are truly happier after major change. Believe that you will be one of those people one day soon, and believe it every day, no matter how difficult it may get at times. Be tough, be strong, and be positive not only for yourself but also for everyone around you.*

A FEW WORDS ABOUT RÉSUMÉS

Good résumés are made up of few words. The best résumés are simple and easy to follow; they should be one page and should communicate exactly the right aspects about you and your career. So, what are the right aspects of a great résumé?

At the top of the résumé in the center, you should list all your pertinent information. Your name, address, e-mail, and phone numbers should be listed in a clear, logical order. All this information should be current without any qualifications or write-in changes. If there are changes, print a new résumé. It's critical that everything on this piece of paper is correct and professional. Sure, the information itself is important, but you can't change the information; it is what it is. You can control the format of your résumé and its professional look and clarity. Make sure all of the voice recordings for the phone numbers you offer are professional, clear, and succinct. I believe that during the search, your voice should be on the recorder versus your children's voice. After you get the job, change the recordings back. Cover every potential touch that could occur during the search with an air of professionalism. You're selling a package here, and you are the package!

Career goals should be listed next. This statement or series of statements describe what's next in your sales career. These should be based on your past accomplishments and what goals and objectives you still seek in your career.

- Over the past several years, my experiences have been related to _____. As I move forward in my sales career, I seek the opportunity to move into _____ and enhance my income potential and level of professionalism.
- As my sales career develops, I seek an opportunity to develop a list of clients who are more professional than my current contacts. I also seek to sell larger projects with greater possibilities to enhance my income potential.
- At this point in my sales career, I seek an opportunity where I would be able to in time begin to manage salespeople and mentor under a sales manager I respect and trust.

These are just some initial ideas as they relate to this subject. Hopefully, you feel the above statements are clear, concise, and informative. Be very careful not to ramble on or paint a picture of the future in your career that is not truly how you feel.

The next phase of your résumé should relate to educational history. This area is also an area to be absolutely honest. List your educational experiences starting with high school, including dates of completion. If you are young enough to change your feelings on this area for the better, do it! Take classes at night or whatever, but don't let your education hold you back from accomplishing your goals in the sales profession. On the other hand, don't let your educational level be the excuse for success in sales. There are plenty of very successful salespeople with a high school education. Make sure you don't use education to cover up another deficiency like the inability to actually sell enough to be successful. A higher education will only give you a chance to prove yourself and perform. But in the end, it still comes down to performance, work ethic, clear thinking, and problem solving coupled with an ability to work with and motivate others. Some of these topics, if not all of them, can be learned only to a certain extent in the classroom; the street is where it happens and true learning takes place.

The next section of your résumé is your employment history. If you have a clear, logical path in your career, you should be very proud of yourself. Clearly disseminate it on your résumé and continue to move forward in the sales profession. For others, the list of past employers makes a little less sense. If you've had 10 jobs in 20 years, I wouldn't list all 10. This is not a fishing expedition. We are not trolling for opportunities that might match up with what we did 15 years ago. I would list the last four jobs or about eight years' worth. Hopefully, those last jobs show a pattern of interest and experience you can build on with your new employer. The distant past is not important anymore. The recent past and the near future are the most important factors at hand. Focus on those!

The next section should be sales training. Potential sales managers love to see that you are already trained and potentially savvy in sales. Any seminars or formal training in sales is important, and you should list this information.

The last section is references. I believe you should list them *with phone numbers* and maybe the type of reference they would offer. One person could be a large project coordination reference. Another could be a character reference on your management abilities. I personally hate the statement "available upon request." To me it says you haven't taken the time to get your act together on references by the time of the résumé printing, and it shows me lack of planning. It also shows me lack of sensitivity of my time if I'm interested in a candidate. I would have to call and get references before I call them. It's another step on my part to hire a candidate. Make it easy for your potential employer to look at your résumé and just call your references. Be as professional and efficient as you can to pave the way for you to be the one who is hired. *Always* call the people you are using as a reference to see whether they would like to be your reference and whether they will support you. Never assume they will support you.

When it comes to sales, I personally don't like to see a list of personal interests. When I see golf on a list of personal interests, I just roll my eyes. I usually think to myself, "Not another salesperson I have to wonder about as to whether he or she is on the golf course this nice afternoon." If you do it to be able to potentially strike a common cord, well, strike a common cord on sales training or your ability to sell the task at hand. If the sales manager is interested in your interests as they relate to entertaining clients and your ability to golf, he or she will ask for that information.

All this information should not go to a second page. I hate two-page résumés. They say to me lack of focus. All a résumé is trying to do is create a need or desire to meet you personally. If you can't create an interest to meet you personally in one page of information, something is wrong. I also like to see white space on the résumé, not that the candidate wanted to single-space everything and get it all in on one page. In this fast-paced environment, a potential sales manager wants to look at clear, concise statements about your abilities, past experiences, and future potential. Achieve the items above in your résumé and give yourself the best chance to obtain a personal interview.

OFF TO GREENER PASTURES

Business careers are sometimes divided into four quarters of approximately 10 years each. In today's business environment, it's hard to imagine having a sales-oriented position with the same company for the entire 40-year period of time. The job interview sooner or later will become a reality during a salesperson's career—most of the time sooner rather than later. Just a brief chapter on the best practices as they relate to interviewing is the goal.

The **handshake**, **initial eye contact**, and remembering ***"the name"*** are critical to starting off on the right foot. Most all sales managers like a firm, well-positioned handshake. Don't miss this opportunity. If the handshake itself doesn't engage correctly, then I believe you should start over and get it right. As you are conducting this handshake, it's important to make direct eye contact and hold it for a second to reinforce it! This eye contact is not to be a glancing blow. It's to be direct and sincere. The last thing to do is remember the name. The name, the name—remember the name. If the interviewer lets you call him "Bob," then fine, but do so only after you begin by calling him Mr. So-and-So.

The idle chitchat is fine on the way back to the interview room; however, when you sit down, continue to sit **straight up and forward**. Energetic, eager sales representatives sit forward. Complacent sales representatives look relaxed and sit down like they needed to take a load off.

As it relates to **dress**, a salesperson should always error to the more formal. Only if the interviewer makes a point of mentioning that it is business casual on the day you interview should you wear business casual. Certainly different parts of the country dictate different understandings of formal. You would like to be overdressed rather than underdressed and try to make up for it all throughout the interview.

Nervousness is common, so be prepared for it. Usually the interviewer will ask whether you would like a glass of water, and you should always say yes. It's not about whether you're thirsty at the time; it's just that if you become thirsty later, you're prepared, and at times, a drink of water can be a welcome break in the heat of battle. Further, I always try to laugh about something together to become relaxed early in the interview. If you are nervous, take a deep breath, or you could say, "I'm sorry I'm a little nervous; this interview is important, and I want to do my best." Also remember that all the interviewers have been trained on the fact that it's their job to make the interviewee relaxed. I know it doesn't help the situation, but it's not totally your fault if you're nervous. Is the fact that the interviewer didn't help you relax the first sign of what type of environment you are getting into?

It's important to have a ***pre-interview plan*** *just like you would before a sales call. Research the company before going into the interview. I'm always amazed at how many sales candidates I interview haven't written down any questions to ask before coming to the interview. The percentage is sky high. Lack of preparation prior to the interview is a total tip off to preparation after the hire. Remember that a great interviewer is looking for small signs that present themselves in the interview process. Any negative signs I ever saw in the* *interview process I blew up 10-fold, and I analyzed whether I could live with those negatives when going forward.* **Write down five to seven questions (not related to compensation in any way) in a nice folder that are well thought out and provide good information for *you* to analyze *their* job.** Interviewing is a two-way street! Be careful about questions related to compensation issues. Greed and self-interest questions don't come off well in interviews, especially early in the process. If the interviewer is good, he or she will present compensation issues on a certain time frame, and it's best to wait until he or she is ready to discus these issues. If the topic doesn't come up in the first interview, I wouldn't bring it up until the second interview. Don't look hungry, greedy, or focused on what you will get before you do anything to deserve it! Place all these issues on the back burner until the interviewer is ready. Some might say that if you don't look hungry or interested in compensation, then the interviewer won't think you are a producer. All I'm saying is that there is a time and place for everything, and this is not the time to talk about compensation unless the interviewer opens up the box.

Behavior-based interviewing is the best interviewing technique used today. All the questions will begin with "Tell me about a time when" or "Give me a specific example when" or "Now, let's talk about a time when it didn't go so well." All the questions will elicit responses that explain real, live examples of when in the past a particular behavior occurred. Past behavior is a great indicator of future behavior. With this in mind, I'm not sure how you would prepare differently other than possibly thinking over situations in the past that might demonstrate good behavior so you are prepared. It's probably just as important to think about situations that didn't go as planned because the interviewer will want you to talk about how you handled these situations as well!

I'm a big believer in showing documentation that displays past performance results: copies of plaques, sales charts with your name on top, and all those types of accolades that show high performance.

Many sales managers are bothered by complacency in their current sales staff. Once salespeople reach an income level that fits in their lifestyle, it's very hard for them to perform at a higher level for any extended amount of time. Questions an interviewer asks about desired income can begin to paint the complacency picture around your situation based on your answers. These managers certainly like to hear that you are not happy with your current living conditions and would work hard to change them or that you have tremendous determination to achieve a certain threshold in income in your career. Maybe before you answer these questions, you should ask some of your own as they relate to what the company's "stars" earn in any given year and base your answer on those responses, always creating value around the higher income targets.

Certainly recap the interview at the end like you would a sales call as to what each participant will accomplish. I believe you should be bold, almost like asking for the order in a way, and ask, "How many candidates are in the hunt for this opportunity?" "How do you think I did today?" "How will the decision be made and in what time frame?" Remember: you're in sales. Salespeople are supposed to be assertive. This sales manager wants professionally assertive salespeople on his or her staff. Play out that role in the interview!

I'm old school, but I still like a handwritten thank you note quickly sent after the interview. Maybe include your favorite sales article that highlights some parameters you live by each and every week. I know this is the era of e-commerce, and a quick e-mail is acceptable. But that's what it is; it's quick, and everyone does it. I always like to see a little more time and effort spent. Make sure your handwriting is clear, correct, and professional. Oftentimes the manager will look at this as an indication of how his or her customers will eventually receive responses from you.

BEGINNING SALES MANAGEMENT (APPENDIX)

Sooner or later, great salespeople will have the opportunity to move into sales management. I offer these last several chapters as a basis for your arrival into this intriguing next step in the sales profession. This subject is the basis for another entire book. It's my hope that these last few chapters will help you arrive, or if you have arrived, I hope these chapters offer reinforcement of what you already may be doing or have experienced.

THE 5 C'S OF SALES MANAGEMENT

Great sales management, as a sales call itself, is also an art form. Until you have arrived on the scene and hung around for a while, the dynamics of this art form is mostly misunderstood. Many who sell well also believe they can manage well. They believe they know how to make it happen, and they simply need to teach others "their" way to success. The problem is that their way isn't always a fit for other people. There are so many aspects associated with their way that some aspects without others just don't add up to the same level of success over time. The manner in which a sales manager implements these aspects into others is fragile and a continuous, ongoing effort. There are some main lifelines to hold onto as you navigate these uncharted waters in the early stages of your sales management career.

Salespeople need to be "cherished." Maybe it's the same about all professions, but salespeople are a different breed of cat. Maybe it's their ego, stress level, or yearning for the forefront or the almighty dollar, but emotions usually run high when a winning salesperson is involved. Cherish your winners. Make them feel special in your verbal interactions and always outwardly appreciate them and their wins *without qualifying them in any way*. Help them feel like they are on "cloud nine" and try to keep them there. If you, as a sales manager, have some winners, *never take them for granted*, always cherish them, and remind them how much they mean to the organization. If they do decide to "jump ship," someday you will be glad you cherished them along the way and that it wasn't an excuse for leaving. Sometimes this cherishing of winners fills their already full egos; make sure that you are always tough on where the line is drawn for them and all the others. *All this cherishing doesn't mean they have any different privileges.* The most difficult part of cherishing is how to cherish losers. I believe that losers need to be totally cherished until they *earn* the title of "loser." Some sales managers believe that some salespeople will become losers, and they stop cherishing long before these salespeople actually achieve loser status. Great sales managers are eternal optimists and believe they can make a winner out of anyone over time. The problem is that the best sales managers realize when they run out of time. They give it their all as it relates to the poor-performing sales representative, but there is an end to the effort, and they judge correctly where this end is, and they are not afraid to take action when the end of the tunnel appears. I believe that a sales manager can modify performance at best. Dramatic transformations of salespeople may occur, but they are usually short lived and their true character appears again in time. The best managers are the ones who perceive the best talent at the beginning and mold them to be the best they can be by cherishing them every day to get the most out of the talent they perceived in the first place. More important, if the talent they perceived in the first place proves to be off base, they are very critical of these perceptions and don't make the same mistake twice. *Cherish away, but always try to do it in private so the others don't start comparing your levels of cherishing.*

Sales mangers must master the art of "cheerleading" as well. Every day, the "you can do it" attitude must shine. The success of sales managers depends on the success of their salespeople, so the best make it all about them. Build your people up with a relentless "you can do it" attitude. Cheerlead them all the way to *their* bank, not yours. Always find a way to build them up in front of their customers as well. *The most important test of this "you can do it" attitude is when it's communicated in front of others.* When reviewing an improvement situation with them, always try to offer two or three positives with a shorter list of negatives you so dearly want to communicate. Don't just come up with these positives to outnumber the negatives either. They have to be legitimate and carry substance. The negatives are a vital part of their growth and your growth together. Great sales managers have such a rapport and respect with their salespeople that these people take the negatives in stride and sincerely believe that these suggestions will help them sell more. Cheerlead these people to achieve their individual best so the group achieves maximum output.

Salespeople need to be consoled. Whether they are coming off a recent loss or a work- or family-related problem, it's important to listen, absorb, and show genuine interest and support. If the subject at hand is work related, it may or may not be your place to suggest solutions. Be careful of the decision you come up with on this subject. Being consoled has nothing to do with offering solutions; make sure you draw the line between the two. It's especially important to draw the line between consoling and suggesting solutions on non-work-related topics. Generally, only console in these situations and be very careful when you cross this line, very careful!

Great sales managers collaborate with their salespeople. When a collaboration is developed, both people have responsibilities. Great sales managers are organized enough to collaborate with their salespeople. Collaboration takes time and effort, and many sales managers either don't have the time because they are so unorganized or feel as though they are "above" certain forms of collaboration with their people and embrace the feeling of "that's their job, not mine"! In some cases the previous statement is on target, but more times than not, *a sales manager's interest in helping a salesperson succeed takes him or her into most any area that will help that salesperson succeed, and these managers create true collaboration with their salespeople. When a sales manager takes on a "nothing is beneath" him or her attitude, true collaboration is developed, and the sales manager and salesperson team that is developed becomes very powerful and productive.* This should not be translated into taking on items for which the salesperson is responsible. It's more of a sharing of efforts to leverage the salesperson's time or that the sales manager takes items that relate to higher authority needs to solving tough problems.

Great sales managers churn their salespeople. Letting people go is the toughest thing any sales manager has to decide upon. Sometimes the decision to let someone go is made long before the words "you're fired" appear. Don't let procrastination enter into this situation. The situation won't get better, the situation won't go away, the situation won't resolve itself, and the situation will eat away at a great sales manager until that salesperson has a job with another company. It's important to give the salesperson in question enough time to succeed. Turnover is very costly in a multitude of respects too many to talk about here. Make sure that you and this person have truly collaborated and that there is nothing you as the sales manager can do to help improve performance. The best sales managers are not above anything that would improve performance to save a failure. But in the end, if the ingredients for success are just not appearing after an acceptable amount of time, decide and move on. Create an environment whereby both parties can move on gracefully if possible. Set a time frame and stick to it so that it becomes just a matter of time before the situation is resolved. It also allows time to search for a replacement as early as possible, which is also important for moving on. The best sales manager also takes on the role of career counselor for a salesperson new to the sales profession. Career guidance is an important part of any sales manager's role, especially as it relates to whether a particular salesperson is cut out for the sales profession.

THE CANDLE AND THE GLASS

We all remember the night we came home from grade school with a couple science experiments to try at home. Do you remember the experiment when your parents lit a candle and set a glass nearby? The candle began to burn bright, and it gave off a radiant glow. Then you were asked to place the glass over the candle and lower it over the flame. The lower you moved the glass, the fainter the flame got until finally the candle went out all together to your amazement.

We all need air to survive, especially salespeople. As salespeople move from good to great, they need more and more air to survive. Even great salespeople need continued doses of air to remain at peak performance. The best salespeople realize they have to be very good at providing their own doses of air if they are going to succeed. They pump themselves up during tough times. They use their wins to propel them forward so they can sit beside Mr. Mo Mentum. They believe they will succeed and use that inner belief to motivate themselves in what seems like a never-ending, long, tough race. But low and behold, along comes some external force that begins to lower the glass on *their* candle. It could be family issues, personal issues, a political environment at the office, a sales slump, a bad sales manager, or lost confidence, and their candle begins to flicker because of lack of air.

The great sales manager reaches for the glass and begins to lift it off the candle. First, he or she realizes what's begun to happen early on because of being perceptive. The sales manager calmly opens a discussion with the salesperson and showers the salesperson with lots of air. "Hey, are you all right?" "I've begin to notice some small things that don't match your character." "I want you to know you have my total support and confidence, and you and I will team up to get back on track." *"Is there anything I could do to change or help you?"* After any of these questions, it's then time to just listen and absorb—don't suggest. Your goal is to lift the glass, not to propose solutions at this point. This is like the information-gathering phase in a sales call; it gets the salesperson talking, drains the well, and exposes the whole iceberg. Only when the well is totally drained or the iceberg is totally exposed do you begin to craft the beginnings of any possible solutions. Begin to decide on the best solution to the problem and chip away at it *with* the salesperson in a systematic fashion with a clear time frame for resolution. During the process, pay close attention to this salesperson, help him or her, and analyze his or her ability to get back on track. Your goal is to get his or her flame to glow again, radiantly. If his or her flame doesn't come back to full strength, try another solution or, if possible, two other solutions, but when it's time to change sales representatives and remain a great sales manager, do it and don't procrastinate. Decide, act, move ahead, take action, and don't make excuses for your inability to act.

Sometimes certain salespeople have a tendency to "politically" lower the glass on other salespeople or support staff. Act on this as well; great teams have no political strife, no dissension, no questioning or wavering from the goal or belief in that goal.

If you've found "the cancer," then eliminate it and watch how brightly all the other candles begin to burn once the cancer is gone. And that overall goal of yours, well, now, achieving it is only a matter of time! It may take a little longer to achieve, but you will achieve it, and you'll feel great when you do—and more important, so will everyone around you!

JOINT SALES CALLS

As you move up in the sales profession, there might be more and more times when you are asked to go with another salesperson on a sales call. It might be because of your experience, it might be because of your expertise, or it might be because your sales manager is out of town and you are the next best option. It might be because you are being molded to possibly become a sales manager some day and this is the first page of your sales manager test. Whatever the case, be proud that you have been asked to help. Let this feeling of being proud last for about five seconds, and then forget about it and get to work.

Believe it or not, the planning of this call is more important than any call you have been on by yourself. When you make calls with two or more mouths present on your side of the table instead of just one, the sales call can get awfully interesting very quickly. There are several very important parameters that must be cast in stone before you venture into this call.

- **Set aside an hour before the call to prepare.** This preplanning may take only 30 minutes, or it might take the whole hour, but don't ever short yourself on the preplanning of these important events in your sales career. Take your pre-call plan form and decide on every specific stage of the call. Decide on who is in charge of that section, how long it will take, and what will be said. It's also important to talk about how the transition will be made to the next phase and obviously who will take charge of the next phase.

- **The group must decide on a leader.** There has to be a leader on joint sales calls. Usually it's the senior person or the person most responsible for the sales call being productive. Whatever the case, the leader is in charge; he or she is the traffic cop for the event. The leader decides when to move on because of time or because of tangents developing in the call that don't relate to the intended mission. Everyone in the call has to respect the wishes of the leader. Copies of the agenda down to the minute are passed out and adhered to strictly.
- **Subtle signs are decided upon between all parties as to when someone needs help.** Everyone needs a part in the call for the sake of growth in the sales profession. But, when a new person needs help, there is a natural way, like eye contact, to ask for help, and then the leader helps out and takes control for a while. It's important to make sure after help is successfully received that the leader gets the call right back on track. *The leader doesn't take over the rest of the call.* A great leader is there to add assistance and then step back again and follow the original plan. There is no excuse for throwing the plan out the window. *Great leaders believe in the plan from the very start and die with the plan 95% of the time.* On **very few occasions** is there justification to wing it and toss the plan into the wind.
- **There are two types of joint sales calls: a "coaching joint sales call" and a "participation joint sales call."** If you are involved in a coaching event and you are the coach, it's vital you do very little talking if any! Your main focus is your salesperson,

not the client. Your goal is not to step in and save the call. It's better to plan the call and let the salesperson conduct the call with no interference. It's probably the most difficult task a sales manager has to do, and many can't do it. *When the two of you arrive in the prospect's office, make sure you sit a little behind your salesperson in relation to the prospect so you are farther away from the prospect than the salesperson. It should be obvious to the prospect that your role is to watch or coach. It will also be obvious to your salesperson that it's his or her game. This positioning will go a long way to set the stage for everyone involved.* The participation sales call is simply one where you plan ahead as to who does what and everyone plays his or her role. Nobody plays anyone else's role, and the leader keeps track of everything.

- **Only go on joint sales calls if you can make a unique difference in the call, either by coaching or participating.** Don't ever go on a sales call without the salesperson responsible for that account. If there is a reason to see an account, take the salesperson and go on the call!
- **Last, but not least, be very careful of the type of involvement you have in the call.** "I'm sure Joe will be happy to follow up on that for you." "Joe can take the lead on that subject." "Joe has done a great deal of work on this already, and _____." "I've seen several situations where Joe has done a great job on these types of issues. He will _____." The salesperson on the account, Joe, must remain the lead for information, follow-up, and decision making or *you just got a new account*!

> *Two heads are better than one! Just think of the power of the team. Clearly define the roles of player and coach and power forward together!*

ASSESSING SALES TALENT

As you begin to move more and more into sales management, it will become more and more important to assess sales talent. Whether you have one member on your sales team or 100, assessing sales potential in sales representatives will consume a great number of your waking *and sleeping* hours! It's a never-ending process and a process that can push even the best sales managers into anxiety overload. It's all about potential as it relates to future production. *Is a particular sales representative at peak production? Will the tailspin just continue, and is it best to "cut bait" right now and reload? Is the sky the limit for this budding star and next year will be again as good, if not even better, as this year? Will this sales rep ever get it and produce any more? Will there be another outburst like the last one and kill all the team atmosphere that has taken so long to create? Does that sales representative think I've got my head in the sand and I don't know that _____? I'm just going to keep so-and-so; I dread the thought of looking, yet again, for a sales representative for that area. Maybe things will get better next year. I couldn't let him or her go and do that to his or her family, at least not at this time of the year. He or she deserved the chance to move into sales, and I'm going to stick with my decision!* On and on and on. Welcome to life in sales management. It's certainly not for the weak at heart.

I'll make some statements for food for thought. Either these statements will reinforce some feelings you already have on this subject or they will be a basis for consideration as you move forward in the world of sales management.

- **Seldom do things get better.** They either remain the same over time or get worse. The tailspin usually does continue, or it levels out at an eventual unacceptable level. Don't fool yourself into believing that this particular case is different and this time "*seldom*" doesn't apply. After the fact, so many sales managers simply say, "I should have decided earlier to _____." *Don't be the "I should have" sales manager!*
- **Will this salesperson keep breaking all the records?** Base your decision on sound facts, not your gut. Was it one large project that showed up last year and will be hard to replace next year? What does this salesperson's sales funnel look like, an empty martini glass? Is he or she aggressively attacking his or her top 30 accounts even though things are all roses right now, or he or she resting on laurels? Is he or she spending all his or her time on dropping another elephant or building a solid base of accounts? Look at the facts and don't get caught up in all the hype.
- **Will this sales rep ever get it?** Most likely not! Most likely, he or she will not change. Most likely you will not change his or her complacency. You might be able to modify it, but will it be enough to make you satisfied? Probably not.
- **Be careful not to be too stubborn about the decisions you have made on hiring sales representatives.** If it was a bad decision, admit it earlier rather than later. Learn from it, retrace your steps, and examine where you went wrong. Decide to move on and reload. But, remember: eventually you will have to

choose some winners along the way if you are going to succeed in sales management. Great sales managers perceive winners before they are hired. They are not always right about their instincts, but they are right much more often than poor sales managers.

- **Great sales managers take potential talent and mold that talent into star status.** They have a knack for bringing the best out of their people. They also have the ability to keep their stars. Poor sales managers have constant turnover. They don't connect with their people to the point where these people wouldn't think of leaving, especially not the stars. It's impossible to build a team when there is constant turnover. It's not *always* the salesperson's fault. After a while, a pattern begins of continual turnover, and before long, the sales manager should be the one on trial!
- **Will it be the last outburst?** Probably not. Get the picture.

> *A great sales manager can modify behavior at best—but, change behavior, probably not—especially not on core issues like complacency, work ethic, attitude, ethics, greed, selfishness, and ego. This category of personality traits was ingrained long before they were hired.*

Thank you for taking the time to read this book. I'm honored you've spent your valuable time. My hope is that my book helps you and your family moving forward. As you know, reading books on sales is vital to your success in sales and life itself! I appreciate the fact that my book was on your list and some other good books that I suggest are listed below. Be passionate about "yearning to learn" and always be proud of your profession, the sales profession. Last, but not least, remember to save your commission dollars not only for any rainy days, but also for all those sunny days at the end of the trail when you have made your last sale.

If you find some of these concepts of value for your company and would like for me to talk about them with your sales team, just email me at *scott@snaconsulting.net.* We could set up a time to talk or meet and see if there is any common ground between us.

First Things First, Stephen Covey

Spin Selling, Neil Rackham

Major Account Sales Strategy, Neil Rackham

Closing Techniques That Really Work, Steve Schiffman

Secrets of Power Negotiating for Salespeople, Roger Dawson

Take Me To Your Leaders, Samuel G. Manfer

Sales Coaching, Linda Richardson

ORDER INFORMATION

Street Smart Selling is available by faxing, calling or emailing an order to Scott Niedermeyer & Associates at the information below:

Scott Niedermeyer & Associates
4506 Deer Park Road
Oconomowoc, WI 53066
Phone: 262-560-1255
Fax: 262-560-1252
Email: *scott@snaconsulting.net*

Please send ____ copies @ $22.50* (shipping included) = $_______
*Five or more copies to same location @ $20.00

Name ____

Address ____

City ___________________________ State _____ Zip _________

Phone _______________________

Credit Card # ______________________________ Exp ___/___

Name on the Card _______________________________________

Card Type ____

Signature ____

Checks Payable to: Scott Niedermeyer & Associates